Manage Your SAP Projects with SAP Activate

Implementing SAP S/4HANA

Vinay Singh

BIRMINGHAM - MUMBAI

Manage Your SAP Projects with SAP Activate

First published: September 2017

Production reference: 1280917

Published by Packt Publishing Ltd.
Livery Place
35 Livery Street
Birmingham
B3 2PB, UK.

ISBN 978-1-78847-036-0

www.packtpub.com

Credits

Author
Vinay Singh

Reviewer
Premkishan H. Chourasia

Acquisition Editor
Prachi Bisht

Content Development Editor
Trusha Shriyan

Technical Editor
Sayali Thanekar

Copy Editors
Ulka Manjrekar
Safis Editing

Project Coordinator
Kinjal Bari

Proofreader
Safis Editing

Indexer
Pratik Shirodkar

Graphics
Kirk D'Penha

Production Coordinator
Shantanu Zagade

Foreword

This book is an outcome of a journey that we (ERP Center at National Centre University, Taiwan) took while doing a PoC (later a project) for S/4HANA. The author being a research scholar at our university was working with various student groups to help them understand the concepts and practices of SAP Activate. We ran through all the phases of SAP Activate and successfully implemented it as per SAP standard recommendations.

Having prior experience on various SAP methodology such as ASAP, SAP Launch, and SAP Activate, the author is able to skillfully guide the readers to apply SAP Activate to accelerate the implementation of various SAP products and solutions. Especially for anyone who is about to kick-start a S/4HANA project, this book is a must read.

Dr Chen, Shiuann-Shuoh

Director of ERP Center, National Central University, Taiwan

About the Author

Vinay Singh is a data science manager at BASF, Germany. He has over 12 years of experience in data warehousing and BI. Before joining BASF, he worked with multiple companies/customers such as SAP, Adobe, Systems, Freudenberg, and T-systems, which gave him a good mix of product development and consulting experience.

His other publications include – *Real-Time Analytics with SAP HANA* (Packt Publishing) and *Creating and Using Advanced DSOs in SAP BW on SAP HANA* (SAP Press). He is a visiting research scholar at the National Central University of Taiwan and conducts guest lectures at Karlsruhe Institute of Technology (Germany).

Acknowledgments

I would like to thank many people who helped me throughout this process. The first mention goes to my wife, Minal, for her understanding of the time I was spending on the book and for her regular feedback.

My special thanks to Premkishan, who is not only the reviewer of the book but also my first project lead. His inputs were very valuable and have helped me to improve the content of the book.

I would also like to thank Prof. Dr. Chen, Shiuann-Shuoh, for the encouragement and support in allowing me to work with student groups from the ERP center, National Central University of Taiwan to develop the content.

Many individuals have provided comments at various stages on portions of this book. I would also like to thank my parents as well as Naveen Rai, Ajeet Ravi, Resham Rai, Nutan Singh, and Poonam Singh for their continuous support and encouragement. I sincerely appreciate the small talks that I had with Frank Strohmaier and Sanjeev Kedarshetty on project management topics and Agile.

Many many thanks to my editors, Trusha Shriyan, Kinjal Bari, Prachi Bisht, and Sayali Thanekar, who worked closely with me and without whom the book would not have been possible. Finally, I would like to appreciate and thank my publishing team and graphics team for their splendid work.

About the Reviewer

Premkishan H. Chourasia is wonderful person. He loves to learn languages and play table-tennis. He is a techno-managerial professional holding 13 plus years of experience and has worked with multiple MNCs.

Premkishan's experience involves working majorly with German, Japanese, British, and Switzerland-based firms.

First of all, I would like to thank my colleague Vinay for choosing me to review this book. While working on this, I was very well-supported by my wife Jyoti who gave me time to review this book and celebrated with enthusiasm on accomplishing it. Needless to say, gratitude to the publication that did really made this happen.

www.PacktPub.com

For support files and downloads related to your book, please visit `www.PacktPub.com`. Did you know that Packt offers eBook versions of every book published, with PDF and ePub files available? You can upgrade to the eBook version at `www.PacktPub.com`and as a print book customer, you are entitled to a discount on the eBook copy. Get in touch with us at `service@packtpub.com` for more details. At `www.PacktPub.com`, you can also read a collection of free technical articles, sign up for a range of free newsletters and receive exclusive discounts and offers on Packt books and eBooks.

`https://www.packtpub.com/mapt`

Get the most in-demand software skills with Mapt. Mapt gives you full access to all Packt books and video courses, as well as industry-leading tools to help you plan your personal development and advance your career.

Why subscribe?

- Fully searchable across every book published by Packt
- Copy and paste, print, and bookmark content
- On demand and accessible via a web browser

Customer Feedback

Thanks for purchasing this Packt book. At Packt, quality is at the heart of our editorial process. To help us improve, please leave us an honest review on this book's Amazon page at https://www.amazon.com/dp/1788470362.

If you'd like to join our team of regular reviewers, you can email us at customerreviews@packtpub.com. We award our regular reviewers with free eBooks and videos in exchange for their valuable feedback. Help us be relentless in improving our products!

To my daughter Nitara—just watching you smile makes me realize that life is beautiful

Table of Contents

Preface

This book is written for SAP project managers, consultants, and SAP solution manager experts who intend to understand and use SAP Activate. It will enable them to use agile techniques in SAP and non-SAP projects with sample projects and best practices.

What this book covers

Chapter 1, *Introduction to SAP S/4HANA*, kick-starts our journey of managing SAP projects with SAP Activate. We start the discussion with an overview of SAP S/4 HANA and its features. We will take a detailed look at existing SAP methodologies and compare it with SAP activate. In this chapter, we will also talk about the three pillars of SAP activate and how it supports the different scenarios. We will conclude the chapter with how design thinking concepts are used in SAP Activate and get access to SAP Activate content.

Chapter 2, *SAP Activate Methodology*, details out the SAP activate methodology, its main characteristics, and structure (in cloud, on-premise, and hybrid). This chapter covers how it handles governance, roles, and various implementation approaches. We will also look at solution validation and model company, but these topics will also be discussed in the upcoming chapters.

Chapter 3, *Use Case Scenario for SAP Activate*, discusses the application scenarios of SAP Activate and talks about the main deliverables of each phase of SAP Activate. We will go through the three scenarios in which SAP Activate can be used (new implementations both on cloud and on-premise, system conversion, and landscape transformations) and learn how SAP Activate methodology guides teams through these scenarios.

Chapter 4, *Understanding Agile and Scrum*, focuses on learning the basic concepts of agile and scrum and tries to see how SAP activate has been developed as the next-generation agile methodology. The discussion is focused on the context of agile and scrum concepts in SAP Activate. We also go through how to set up an agile project and how to scale it. The intention is not to go into the details of agile and scrum, but rather correlate and understand SAP activate in the context of agile.

`Chapter 5`, *Sample Projects*, covers how the concepts of agile work in SAP projects. We will take multiple examples from various real-time projects and see how capturing and documenting user requirements and creating a product backlog (all from a SAP project perspective) can be done. We take a closer look at the various phases of SAP Activate and how agile concepts are used in these phases. Industry best practices are also shared during discussion of various concepts.

What you need for this book

We would need the following things:

- Internet access
- Access to SAP solution manager system (720 release)

Who this book is for

This book is intended for project managers, consultants, and SAP solution manager experts who intend to understand and practice SAP activate framework. It will enable them to use agile techniques in SAP projects with sample projects.

Conventions

In this book, you will find a number of text styles that distinguish between different kinds of information. Here are some examples of these styles and an explanation of their meaning.

Code words in text, database table names, folder names, filenames, file extensions, pathnames, dummy URLs, user input, and Twitter handles are shown as follows: "A `JAM ()` group, "SAP Launch implementation methodology for cloud solution", was created to help partners."

New terms and **important words** are shown in bold. Words that you see on the screen, for example, in menus or dialog boxes, appear in the text like this: "Quality Gates are also included in SAP Launch for the four phases of methodology (**Prepare phase** | **Project Verification; Realize Phase** | **Solution Acceptance; Verify Phase** | **Readiness Acceptance and Launch Phase** | **Go-live**)."

Warnings or important notes appear like this.

 Tips and tricks appear like this.

Reader feedback

Feedback from our readers is always welcome. Let us know what you think about this book-what you liked or disliked. Reader feedback is important for us as it helps us develop titles that you will really get the most out of. To send us general feedback, simply email feedback@packtpub.com, and mention the book's title in the subject of your message. If there is a topic that you have expertise in and you are interested in either writing or contributing to a book, see our author guide at www.packtpub.com/authors.

Customer support

Now that you are the proud owner of a Packt book, we have a number of things to help you to get the most from your purchase.

Downloading the color images of this book

We also provide you with a PDF file that has color images of the screenshots/diagrams used in this book. The color images will help you better understand the changes in the output. You can download this file from https://www.packtpub.com/sites/default/files/downloads/ManageYourSAPProjectswit hSAPActivate_ColorImages.pdf.

Errata

Although we have taken every care to ensure the accuracy of our content, mistakes do happen. If you find a mistake in one of our books-maybe a mistake in the text or the code-we would be grateful if you could report this to us. By doing so, you can save other readers from frustration and help us improve subsequent versions of this book. If you find any errata, please report them by visiting `http://www.packtpub.com/submit-errata`, selecting your book, clicking on the **Errata Submission Form** link, and entering the details of your errata. Once your errata are verified, your submission will be accepted and the errata will be uploaded to our website or added to any list of existing errata under the Errata section of that title. To view the previously submitted errata, go to `https://www.packtpub.com/books/content/support` and enter the name of the book in the search field. The required information will appear under the **Errata** section.

Piracy

Piracy of copyrighted material on the internet is an ongoing problem across all media. At Packt, we take the protection of our copyright and licenses very seriously. If you come across any illegal copies of our works in any form on the internet, please provide us with the location address or website name immediately so that we can pursue a remedy. Please contact us at `copyright@packtpub.com` with a link to the suspected pirated material. We appreciate your help in protecting our authors and our ability to bring you valuable content.

Questions

If you have a problem with any aspect of this book, you can contact us at `questions@packtpub.com`, and we will do our best to address the problem.

1
Introduction to SAP S/4HANA

Let's kick-start the journey of managing SAP projects with SAP Activate. We will start the discussion with an overview of SAP S/4HANA and its features. We will take a detailed look at existing SAP methodologies and compare them with SAP Activate. In this chapter, we will also talk about the three pillars of SAP Activate, and how it supports different scenarios. We will conclude the chapter with how design thinking concepts are used in SAP Activate and getting access to the SAP Activate content.

S/4HANA in a nutshell

Data volumes are growing, and the pace of this growth is unprecedented. The volume, variety, velocity, and veracity of these data coming from the sensor, social media, and other sources are far outstripping traditional business suite systems. We are living in the digital world and the exponential growth in digital information cannot be handled by just upscaling our infrastructure or revamping existing processes, as this will complicate the solution.

The paces of underlying hardware architecture advancement and computing power are way faster, and to take advantage, we need to adapt them and redesign the business suite for the digital world.

So, SAP has rewritten the complete suite, which is named SAP S/4HANA. SAP S/4HANA promises that customers can completely reimagine their business models, processes, and decision making with an enriched end user experience. Run simple in the digital economy and drive instant value across the organization.

SAP S/4HANA is a real-time enterprise resource management suite for digital businesses. It is built on the advanced in-memory platform, SAP HANA, and offers a personalized, consumer-grade user experience with SAP Fiori. Deployable on the cloud or on-premise, SAP S/4HANA can drive instant value across all lines of business, irrespective of the industry or business size:

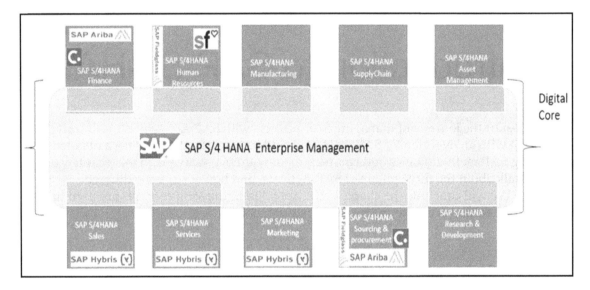

S/4HANA as a core of the next generation of SAP offers

The salient features of SAP S/4HANA

SAP S/4HANA is built on SAP HANA, so it has all the capabilities of this powerful data management and application platform, including predictive analysis, real-time decision supports, and advanced text mining. Let's take a quick look at a few of the salient features of SAP S/4HANA, listed as follows:

- Can be deployed on-premise or on a cloud or hybrid model
- Contains simplified data models, reduced tables, and footprints
- Is fully integrated with the SAP HANA cloud platform, allowing organizations to build faster and more cost effective business applications
- SAP S/4HANA increases the efficiency of enterprise processes by embedding analytics in the transactional context and by removing visibility blackouts caused by batch processing

- Overlaps and redundancy, including earlier multiple add-on applications surrounding a core (for example, SAP ERP, SAP CRM, and SAP SRM), have been completely removed in SAP S/4HANA
- A brandnew user experience is delivered to improve the productivity and satisfaction of business users, bringing the interface up to a consumer-grade experience on any device
- A database that supports S/4HANA (SAP HANA) can handle both OLTP and OLAP processing from a single model, and therefore, we do not need to move transactional data to a separate system

So, how can SAP Activate help us to get a quick jumpstart with SAP S/4HANA?

One of the first questions that should come to our mind is, "How does SAP Activate as a methodology help make the SAP S/4HANA implementation faster?"

The answer to the preceding question lies in the following capabilities provided by SAP Activate:

- Provides you with tools needed for an assisted implementation
- Facilitates sample reference solutions containing organizational and master data
- Clears confusion over methodologies by providing one methodology
- Suitable for any type of deployment (in terms of size, cloud/premise)
- Offers continuous support in adaptation of latest innovations

Existing SAP methodology - SAP ASAP 8.0 and SAP Launch

SAP already had multiple methodologies prior to SAP Activate, for example, **Accelerated SAP** (**ASAP**) for on-premise and SAP Launch for the cloud. Before we go ahead with the SAP Activate methodology, let's quickly review and summarize the SAP ASAP methodology and the SAP Launch methodology. This will help us to quickly find the differences between the three and help us to better understand SAP Activate offerings.

The ASAP methodology

ASAP provides a proven, comprehensive, repeatable, and rich implementation methodology to streamline projects. It is a phased, delivery-oriented methodology that minimizes risk and reduces the total cost of implementation. It supports project teams with templates, tools, questionnaires, and checklists, including guidebooks and accelerators.

There was a lot of enhancement with each version of ASAP; here we will consider the latest version, ASAP 8.0.

The salient key features of SAP ASAP are:

- It brings a shift in focus from project to program value
- It has industry standard aligned project management processes and guidelines (PMI); ASAP 8.0 has also adapted to agile, irises, and design thinking built-in guidance
- Transparency of value delivery through consistent business case reflection
- It delivers content rich implementation accelerators, templates, and guides that help reduce the total cost of implementation
- It enables efficient project governance and quality management
- It covers the entire project life cycle from evaluation through delivery to post-solution management and operations
- ASAP WBS is streamlined into three levels with prescriptive delivery attributes (accountability, delivery mode, and so on)

Let's take an example of an implementation project and see how the ASAP methodology can be used for it. An implementation project typically has the following ASAP phases and workstreams:

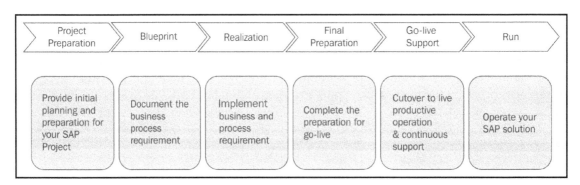

ASAP implementation roadmap

The implementation roadmap has six phases:

- **Project preparation**: The project is formally initiated and planning is well under way. In this phase, it is expected to achieve the following tasks:
    - Identify project objective
    - Build a capable project team
    - Get buy-in from stakeholders and senior management

- **Business blueprint**: The conceptual design of solution happens in this phase, after collecting all the requirements. It results in (varies if we are using agile ASAP 8.0 or standard ASAP):
    - Baseline build (in case of agile ASAP)
    - Project backlog (in case of agile ASAP)
    - Detailed documentation of results gathered during requirement workshops (in case of standard ASAP)

- **Realization**: The solution is built and the integration testing is done. We also plan the performance test in this phase. It results in:
    - Baseline configuration
    - Fine-tuned systems
    - Completed testing and integration
    - Emphasized knowledge transfer

- **Final preparation**: End user training is conducted. A final check is performed before cutover to the new system solution. It is expected that the following outcomes are delivered:
    - End user training
    - Mock rehearsals are successful
    - Workload testing is complete

- **Go-live support**: The solution receives confirmation, ongoing support is in place, and the project is closing.

- **Run**: The operability of the solution is ensured.

The ASAP methodology is structured in workstreams. Each workstream has a number of deliverables that are to be produced in each phase. Some of the key project workstreams are as follows:

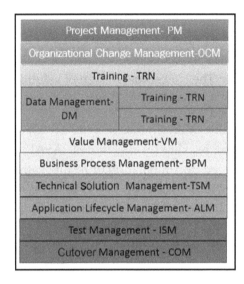

ASAP—Key project workstreams

The SAP Launch methodology (Implementation methodology for the cloud)

The SAP Launch methodology was launched as a replacement (rebranded) for the BizX methodology for cloud implementation in August 2014. It was launched as the methodology to be applied universally across all SAP SAAS implementation. It describes the various implementation activities that need to be performed and the resulting deliverables.

The salient key features of SAP Launch are:

- The core concept of SAP Launch is the "Let us guide you" approach, which is a complete contrast to the traditional approach of, "Can I take your order?"
- A `Jam ()` group, "SAP Launch implementation methodology for cloud solution", was created to help partners.
- Sample project management templates were introduced to help customers and partners jumpstart their projects. The templates also include (checklist for go-live, project closure templates, project preparation **Quality Gates** (**Q-Gate**) acceptance document for each phase and others).
- Quality Gates are also included in SAP Launch for the four phases of methodology (**Prepare phase** | **Project Verification**; **Realize Phase** | **Solution Acceptance**; **Verify Phase** | **Readiness Acceptance and Launch Phase** | **Go-live**).
- The solution-specific delivery toolkits complement the SAP Launch methodology by providing content such as workshop presentations and project accelerators. The contents of the delivery toolkits guide consultants and customers on how tasks are executed for a specific SAP solution. More specific examples of what you might find in a delivery toolkit are the project kickoff workshop presentation and the project schedule template.
- SAP Launch implementation methodologies are harmonized across the success factors, Ariba, cloud for the customer, business bydesign, cloud for travel, and expense solutions.

SAP Launch is a very prescriptive and predictable methodology that is lean and fast, while at the same time it incorporates the iterative and agile approach where it makes sense, like with configuration and testing. This allows us to lead with best practices, yet involve the customer in the configuration and testing cycles to ensure that the solution fits their business.

As we dive into the SAP Launch methodology, we'll notice that there are four phases of the implementation project lifecycle, including prepare, realize, verify, and launch:

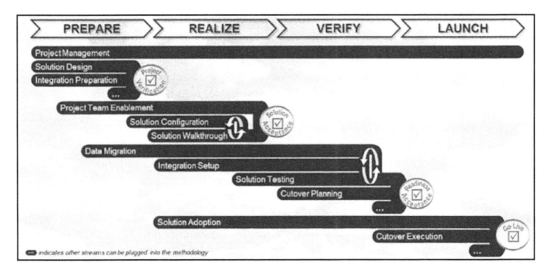

Phases in SAP Launch methodology

The following are the phases in the SAP Launch methodology:

- **Streams**: The main components of the methodology are streams. Streams are collections of tasks required to achieve one or many deliverables. Streams can span many phases (as can be seen in the preceding diagram, for example, the project management stream spanning across all the four phases and solution adoption spanning across realize, verify, and launch).

- **Q-Gates**: The streams are grouped into milestones called Quality Gates. The examples are the solution acceptance Q-Gates and go-live Q-Gates. Quality Gates are executed to confirm that all stakeholders of the implementation project agree that specific deliverables meet the requirements and consequently that the project can continue. They also help maintain the expectation and make sure that the project is heading in the right direction. Points undertaken as a part of Q-Gates also act as an agreement between both the project team and the steady state/release management team. They help in taking objective decisions.

- **Ellipsis**: The streams that show an ellipsis (...), for example, which can be seen after cutover planning in the preceding diagram, indicate that other services/streams can be connected, depending on the customer's business requirements. For example, if a cloud for customer implementation has custom content in scope, then the extensibility stream would be plugged into the methodology.

The phases, streams, and Q-Gates establish the sequence of the activities. Let's dive deeper and take a closer look at the deliverable of each stream.

Project verification Q-Gate deliverables

All the deliverables for project verification Q-Gate are completed in the prepare phase:

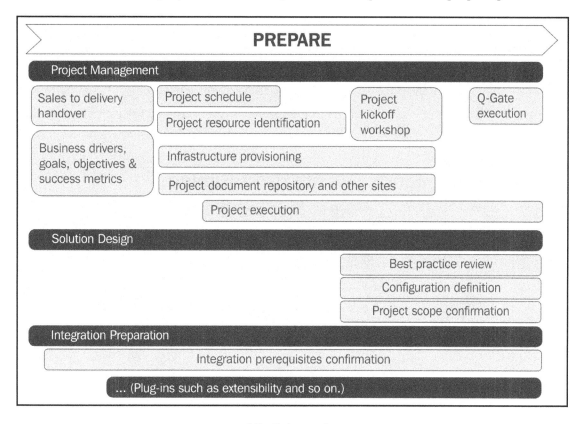

Deliverables in prepare phase

Let's see what is done or expected to be done in streams that are part of this Q-Gate. The project management stream is the deliverables for this stream that start with the handover from the sales team to the services delivery team. The two teams together review the **statement of work** (**SOW**) scope, business drivers, goals, objectives, and relevant success metrics.

Once done, the project manager, along with the customer, finalizes the project schedule, identifies project resources, procures tenant(s), creates the project document repository, and initiates the project status calls/reports. The project is formally kicked off onsite or remotely with the entire team via a workshop:

- **Solution design stream**: The best practices for the to-be business processes are reviewed with the customer, and configuration values are acquired. The project scope is finalized and confirmed in this stream. If the project scope varies from the statement of work, then a change order is executed.
- **Integration preparation**: The prerequisites for integration, security, and infrastructure are prepared by the team. If there is data replication required, the necessary mapping is done.

The project verification Q-Gate confirms that all stakeholders agree on the implementation scope before proceeding with the project.

Solution acceptance Q-Gate deliverables

The deliverables for the solution acceptance Q-Gate are spread over the prepare and realize phases:

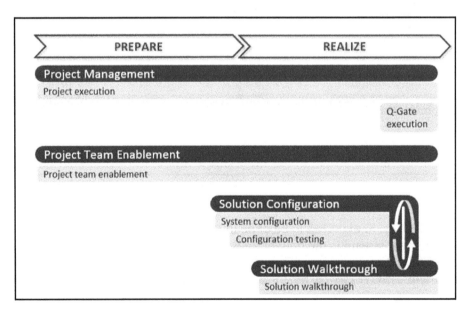

Solution acceptance Q-Gate deliverables

Here, the deliverables are focused on the realization of the agreed upon scope within the SAP solution. Let's see what is done or expected to be done in streams that are part of this Q-Gate:

- **Project management stream**: The project execution deliverable continues as the project manager continues with project status meetings, status reports, and risk management.
- **Project team enablement stream**: As soon as the project initiation happens, the enablement begins, as project team members receive numerous details to prepare for the project and work with the solution. Some of the enablement is delivered via workshops.
- **Solution configuration stream**: In this stream, the system is configured and tested using sample customer data. This includes the configuration of any relevant mobile devices and connections to external service providers.
- **Solution walkthrough stream**: It is used to demonstrate to the customer how his end-to-end process will look within his system. Many times, due to unavailability of all the components, a conceptual walkthrough can also be presented to the customer.

An agile approach allows for several iterations of solution configuration, testing, and walkthrough prior to executing the solution acceptance Q-Gate.

Readiness acceptance Q-Gate deliverables

The deliverables for the readiness acceptance Q-Gate are completed throughout the realize and verify phases. Some data migration activities begin as early as the prepare road:

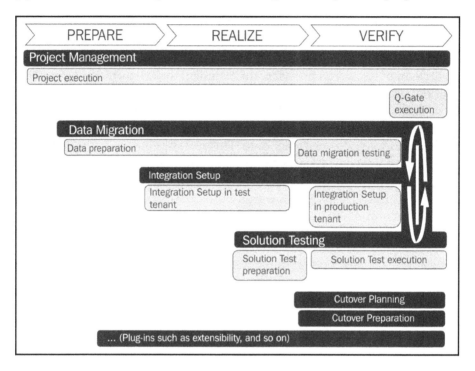

Readiness acceptance Q-Gate deliverables

The readiness acceptance Q- Gate is done once the project team decides that the system, resources or people, and data are ready to proceed with the cutover into the production tenant:

- **Project management stream**: The project execution deliverable is repeated as the project manager continues with project status meetings, status reports, and risk management.
- **Data migration stream**: The data is first extracted from the legacy system and cleansed, then Loaded for testing.
- **Integration setup stream**: It's started in the test tenant. Once the solution testing deliverables are successfully completed, then the setup is repeated in the production tenant.

- **Solution testing stream**: This begins with the customer preparing all the testing documentation. Then, the customer fully tests all end-to-end scenarios using migrated data. This should include analytics, forms, user access, integration, and custom solution extensions.
- **Cutover planning stream**: The project team begins to prepare for the cutover by identifying and scheduling the necessary tasks and resources.

An example of a plugin for the readiness acceptance Q-Gate is when a partner builds a custom solution extension for SAP cloud for travel and expense.

Here again, an agile approach allows for several iterations of data migration, integration set-up, and solution testing prior to executing the readiness acceptance Q-Gate. All testing issues must be resolved or an alternative solution identified before completing the Q-Gate.

Go-live Q-Gate deliverables

Deliverables for Go-live Q-Gate are primarily completed during the verify and launch phases. Some solution adoption activities are executed in the realize phase:

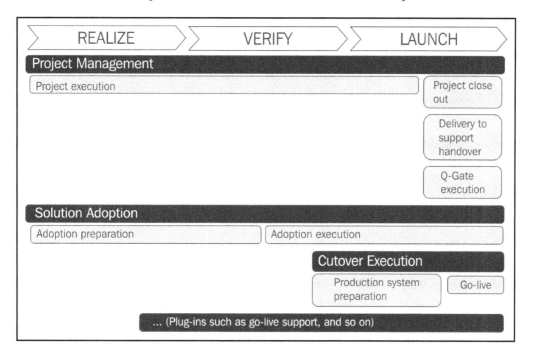

Go-live Q-Gate deliverables

It is the last Q-Gate of the launch phase and occurs at the end:

- **Project management stream**: In addition to the daily project execution, toward the end of the project, the service delivery hands the customer over to SAP support and closes out the project.
- **Solution adoption stream**: In this stream, the customer prepares the transition plan that will be used to roll out the new solution within the organization and with other impacted parties. This includes activities to train users, initiate the productive use of the new solution, and push adoption within the organization.
- **Cutover execution stream**: This delivers a production system that is ready for real transactions. Once go-live Q-Gate is executed, operational transactions are entered and processed in the production environment. Additional purchases by customers (such as go-live support and training) can be also plugged into the methodology as a stream.

Q-Gates in the SAP Launch methodology

The workstreams in SAP Launch are structured into following Quality Gates (as shown in the following image):

- **Project verification**: This Q-Gate ensures that all stakeholders agree on the implementation project scope
- **Solution acceptance Q- Gate**: At the end of the realize phase, the solution acceptance Q-Gate confirms that all stakeholders agree that the demonstrated business processes meet the implementation project requirements and that all configuration questions are addressed
- **Readiness acceptance Q-Gate**: This is when all stakeholders agree that the systems, data, and people are ready to execute cutover

Go-live Q-Gate confirms with all stakeholders that the cutover is complete and the organization is ready to use and support the new solution productively:

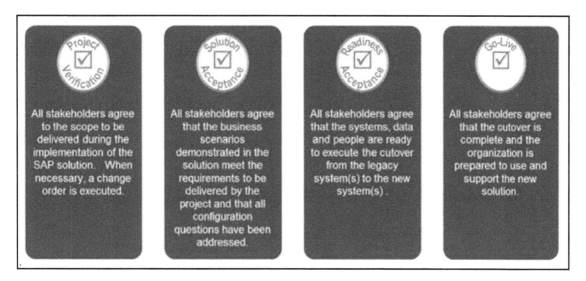

Q-Gates in SAP Launch methodology

Is SAP Launch agile?

SAP Launch is an agile methodology with a little of the waterfall method sprinkled throughout. It uses a very prescriptive and predictable methodology that is lean and fast, while at the same time it incorporates the iterative and agile approaches where it makes sense, like with configuration and testing. This allows us to lead with best practices yet involve the customer in the configuration and testing cycles to ensure that the solution fits their business.

Introduction to SAP Activate and its three pillars

The SAP Activate methodology is a modular and agile framework, which can be used for the following purposes:

- Implementation or migration of SAP systems (with additional focus on SAP S/4HANA)
- A unique combination of SAP best practices, methodology, and guided configuration

- System conversion or a transformation of a larger landscape
- It is the fastest way to simplify your operations with or without SAP S/4HANA

The salient features of SAP Activate are as follows:

- It delivers ready-to-run business processes optimized for SAP S/4HANA with a reference solution
- It has a set of tools for an assisted implementation, covering everything from the initial implementation of a project to running in a production environment and beyond
- It accelerates the initial implementation of SAP S/4HANA and is designed for continuous innovation
- It is the combination of SAP best practices, tools for an assisted implementation, and an agile methodology to simplify the adaptation of SAP S/4HANA
- It facilitates different starting points for customers to move to S/4HANA—new implementation, system conversion, and landscape transformation
- It uses a single methodology for all deployment modes—cloud, premise, and hybrid

Three pillars

SAP best practices, guided configuration, and SAP Activate methodology form the three pillars for SAP Activate, with each bringing special capabilities along with it. In the following diagram, we have jotted down some of the key capabilities that each of these provides to SAP Activate:

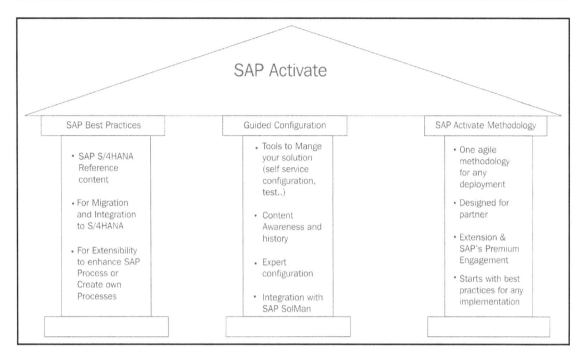

Three pillars of SAP Activate

Let's go a step further and see how these three pillars (SAP Activate overall) support customers' adoption scenarios (details of scenarios are discussed separately):

	New implementation	System conversion	Landscape transformation
SAP Activate - best practices	Supported	Migration and cloud integration	Supports use cases, such as migration and cloud integration, company code carves out
SAP Activate - methodology	Supported	Supported	Supported
SAP Activate - guided configuration	Supported	Not applicable	Applicable if SAP best practices are used for implementation

Table: Three pillars supporting different scenarios

There are three scenarios for the transition to SAP S/4HANA. Let's see the three scenarios and find out the innovation that SAP Activate brings with it for these scenarios.

A new implementation

For a new implementation, where the customer is implementing a new SAP S/4HANA system with initial data load, SAP Activate brings in innovations, and the mentioned innovations can be discovered in the discover phase of SAP Activate:

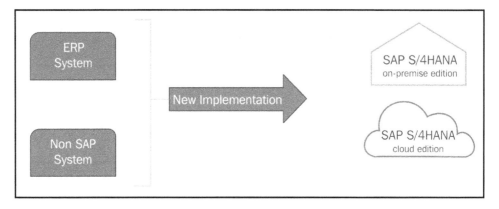

Customer implementing a new SAP S/4HANA system

Let's see phase by phase how SAP Activate supports a customer's implementation of a new SAP S/4HANA system.

SAP Activate's discover phase lets you try and experience the digital business processes offerings:

Innovations delivered with SAP Activate for a new implementation to SAP S/4HANA:

- Preconfigured trial role-based self-led evaluation of SAP S/4HANA based on model company
- Utilizing SAP Fiori user experience
- Integrated help functionality embedded into the product
- Free, click-through license for customers and prospects
- For cloud and on-premise

For the prepare and explore phase of SAP Activate, SAP has delivered the following innovation (for new implementation); this allows customers to start with a model company:

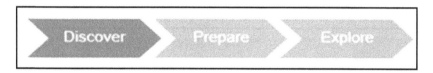

- Prepare setup of projects, install—SAP HANA DB (with applications core), SAP S/4HANA, and Fiori UIs
- Explore ready-to-run business and integration processes optimized for SAP S/4HANA leveraging preconfigured enterprise structure and predefined master data
- Enterprise template to support multiple countries in one client
- Includes **International Financial Reporting Standards (IFRS)**
- Embedded into the standard product shipment of SAP S/4HANA

For the realize phase of SAP Activate, SAP has delivered the following innovation (for new implementation); this simplifies customers, scoping and configuration activities:

- Helps realize solution scoping and scope activation
- Guided configuration allows customers to work with SAP best practices

- User adaptation is a self-service configuration enabling customers to view and change basic settings, such as organization structure
- Expert configuration option available to help customer adapts to SAP model companies and add additional processes as needed
- Predefined mappings to target business objects; this makes the task of landscape transformation easier
- Support for initial data migration (for new implementation scenarios)
- Best practices for integration, for example, integration between SAP ERP HCM and success factors employee central

For the deploy phase of SAP Activate, SAP has delivered the following innovation; this simplifies customers, onboarding and deployment activities:

- Embedded learning and documentation for simple onboarding of end users
- Role-based learning content
- Guided tour to jumpstart the onboarding process for new users
- Context-sensitive screen help

For the run phase of SAP Activate, SAP has delivered the following innovation, which is integrated with solution manager 7.2, to ease the operate, monitor, and support phases:

- SAP solution manager integration for operations, monitoring, and support
- Continuous innovation with content lifecycle management
- With SAP solution manager 7.2, SAP best practices provide reference content for process models, project implementation guidance, and configuration documentation through WBS for each deployment scenario

System conversion

Complete conversion of an existing SAP business suite system to SAP S/4HANA is basically the use case where the customer does not want to go for a new implementation but rather just convert the existing system to SAP S/4HANA:

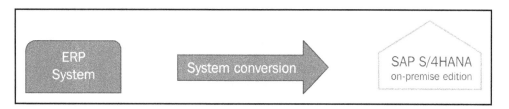

System conversion

For system conversion, SAP Activate brings in the following innovation, which runs through various phases that enable customer to experience trial (in discover), technical preparation steps, test conversion (prepare and explore), functional conversion and cutover (realize), reference content (realize), onboard and deploy (deploy), and operate, monitor, and support (run):

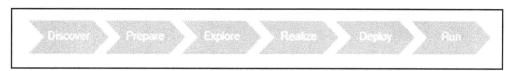

- Role-based self-led evaluation of SAP S/4HANA based on preconfigured business scenarios in trial systems
- Step-by-step guided system conversion with technical preparation and test conversion, with migration best practices based on optimized migration tools for SAP S/4HANA
- Best practices for integration, for example, integration between SAP ERP HCM and success factors employee central
- SAP solution manager integration for operations, monitor, and support
- Context-sensitive screen help
- With SAP solution manager 7.2, SAP best practices provide reference content for process models, project implementation guidance, and configuration documentation through WBS for each deployment scenario

Landscape transformation

This is the use case when a customer wants to consolidate their existing regional SAP business suite landscape into one global SAP S/4HANA system. Selective innovation from the preceding two scenarios (new implementation and system conversion) can serve the purpose of this scenario as well, depending on the requirements, such as integration content:

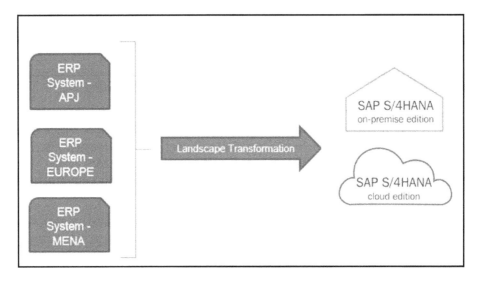

Landscape transformation

As discussed earlier, the following are the three scenarios for the transition to SAP S/4HANA. Let's see how the SAP Activate methodology provides support for all deployment approaches and what the major improvements from ASAP 8.0 and SAP Launch are.

A quick reminder: The SAP Activate methodology is designed to succeed all variants of ASAP and SAP Launch. The following table depicts this:

Scenarios	Earlier	Now	Supported implementation
New implementation	ASAP 8.0	The SAP Activate methodology for on-premise edition	• SAP S/4HANA on-premise edition • SAP business suite
	SAP Launch	The SAP Activate methodology for on cloud edition	• SAP S/4HANA on cloud edition, for example, marketing • Ariba, C4C, and SFSF
System conversion	NA	The SAP Activate methodology for S/4HANA system conversion	• SAP business suite
Landscape transformation	NA	The SAP Activate methodology for S/4HANA landscape transformation	• SAP S/4 HANA on-premise edition • SAP S/4HANA on cloud edition, for example, marketing

Table: The SAP Activate methodology is designed to succeed all variants of ASAP and SAP Launch

The major improvements can be summarized as follows:

- 10 or less key deliverables per phase, thus easier access to key guides and accelerators
- Leverage guided configuration
- Reduced project lifecycle; only four phases

- Enhanced planning and strategy workshop for SAP S/4HANA to guide the customer through the decision and planning process:

SAP Activate	Maps to ASAP	Maps to SAP Launch
Project management	PM:Project Management ALM: Application Lifecycle Management	Project Management
Application: Design & configuration	BPM:Business Process Management(including ROEFW)	Solution design, solution configuration,solution walkthrough
Application:Testing	ISM:Test Management	Solution Testing
Application:Integration	TSM:Technical Solution Management(Integration Design & Environment setup)	Integration preparation Integration setup
Application:Solution Adoption	VM:Value Management OCM:Organization Change Management TRN:Training (end user)	Solution Adaption(part)
Application:Customer Team Enablement	TRN:Training(project team)	Project Team Enablement
Custom code Extensions	BPM:Business Process Management	-NA-
System & Data Migration	DM – Data Migration DA – Data Archiving COM – Cutover Management	Data Migration Cutover planning Cutover Execution
Technical Architecture & Infrastructure	TSM –Technical Solution Management ALM – Application Lifecycle Management	-NA-
Transition to Operations	TSM –Technical Solution Management (incident management change control Management helpdesk process) ALM – Application Lifecycle Management(operation standards for process and people)	Solution Adaption

Mapping SAP workstream's Activate to ASAP and SAP Launch

Design thinking in SAP Activate

What is design thinking?

- A human-centric approach for solving complex problems by generating new ideas, design thinking is for everyone who wants to solve complex problems or create innovative products.
- Design thinking brings an outside-in perspective that helps us understand the goals and needs of our end users and customers, by which we can draw inspiration and insights that help us see new opportunities and drive solutions.

- One of the characteristics of design thinking is to rapidly come up with non-coded prototypes that illustrate ideas and drive conversations. These prototypes are used to validate solution concepts with end users as well as with technical experts.

So, the solution iteratively gets to this optimum that balances the three aspects equally.

The ingredients for design thinking are as follows:

- Combining diverse **people**
- In a creative **space**
- With an iterative **approach**

Design thinking is a technique that (also like many other areas) SAP Activate leverages for user-centric results in multiple contexts. Therefore, design thinking nicely complements SAP Activate:

- Design thinking in SAP Activate lets us focus on a few of the areas where it can be used. We will take a look at a few of the areas; it is not restricted to only these areas, and readers can explore other areas in other phases as well.
- Some of the needs during requirement analysis can be easily tackled by design thinking. For example, collecting requirements from stakeholders and end users and understanding and defining functional requirements.
- In order for project scoping to have better alignment with your stakeholders and scope project in the right way, you can again use design thinking (full or design thinking inspired workshop for project scoping). It will help with benefits such as creating a mission statement for the project; establishing collaboration across the different lines of businesses and stakeholders for the project; identifying the stakeholders and sponsors of the project.
- For business process design when we are challenged with designing a new, or redesigning an existing, business process, design thinking can always be of help. The design thinking workshop can help us to quickly gather knowledge about the "as-is" of the process and help to develop the "to-be". It also helps to build momentum with the customer to raise the acceptance of the new process and get the buy-in from different stockholders.
- For IT architecture design similar to business process design, one needs to quickly gather knowledge about the "as-is" situation of the IT landscape before working on the "to-be" IT landscape. Similarly, it also helps to build momentum with the customer to raise the acceptance of the new IT landscape and get the buy-in from different stockholders.

You can conduct the design thinking session and then transfer the outcomes for all the preceding activities to the SAP Activate templates.

Accessing SAP Activate content

Content for SAP Activate is available in SAP Jam and SAP solution manager. Methodology content can be navigated inside the roadmap viewer tool. In the next section, let's see how we can do so.

Accessing via roadmap viewer

Roadmap viewer can be partially accessed without any special credentials; to see all the content, one would require an s-user id for it. Roadmap viewer is accessible via `https://go.support.sap.com/roadmapviewer/`:

Roadmap viewer

Types of roadmaps

SAP Activate offers general methodologies that can be used as a generic methodology irrespective of product/solution, and also product specific guidance for implementing specific solutions:

- **General methodologies**: Provide framework and approach for running a project across a range of solutions.
- **Product specific**: SAP S/4HANA, SAP HANA technology platform, and SAP solution manager provide guidance for implementation of specific products. The search option facilitates the search for content within the roadmap viewer. The terminologies used at the roadmap viewer are as follows:
  - **Phases**: Stage of the project, at the end of which a Quality Gate exists to verify the completion of the deliverables.
  - **Deliverable**: A tangible or intangible product or service produced as a result of the project that is intended to be delivered to a customer. Several deliverables are included within a workstream.
  - **Task**: Work to be performed; a deliverable has one or more tasks.
  - **Accelerators**: A document, template, pre-built content, or a web link that helps reduce the implementation time.
  - **Workstreams**: The progressive completion of tasks completed by different groups within a company that is required to finish a single project. It is a collection of related deliverables.

- **Services**: Grouping of deliverables in transition to S/4HANA on the premise roadmap that belong to the same services:

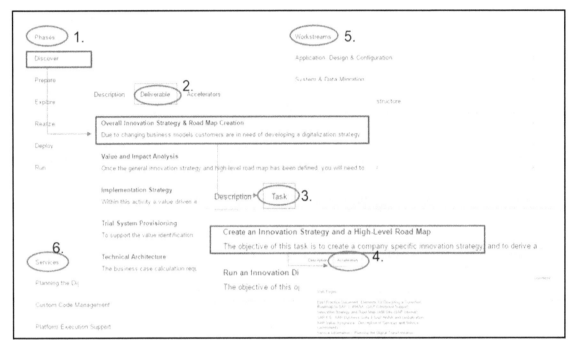

Terminology used in the roadmap viewer

Let's travel through some of the options in the roadmap. You can choose any of the roadmaps, depending on your need; here I chose SAP S/4HANA just to show you the details:

1. Choose the roadmap type (here I chose **SAP S/4HANA**):

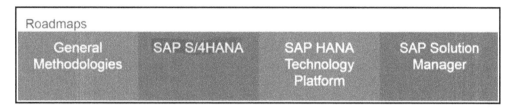

Roadmap type

2. Then, choose the delivery method, **On Cloud** or **On Premise** (I chose **On Cloud**). It shows the **Available Roadmaps**. You can select the roadmap you want to see (I chose **SAP Activate: Implement and Configure SAP S/4 HANA Finance Cloud**):

Roadmaps—Choose the delivery method

3. It takes you to the main page of the chosen roadmap:

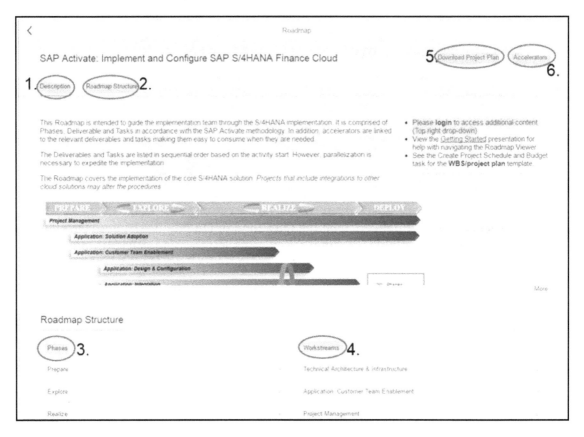

Main page of the chosen roadmap

4. We can traverse through various tabs on the roadmap main page (1, 2, 3, 4, 5, and 6) to find out more about the various options. With **Download Project Plan**, we can download a template project plan and use it.

5. Clicking on **Accelerators** shows all the relevant accelerators for the roadmap. By default, the accelerators are grouped by phase; by clicking on it, the view can be changed, and the view will be in the group by workstream:

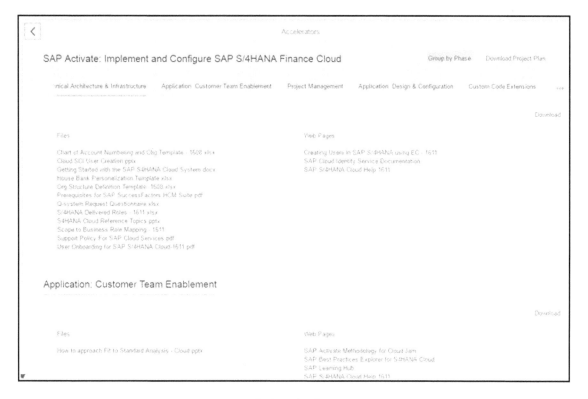

Accelerators in roadmaps

6. The view can be toggled by clicking on **Group by Phase** and we can get the view of **Group by Workstream**:

Accelerator—toggled and Group by Workstream

We can explore various tabs and options available on the roadmap and use it as per requirement.

The home page of the roadmap viewer, `https://go.support.sap.com/roadmapviewer/#`, has the following options to **Learn More**. You can explore more from the following two tabs:

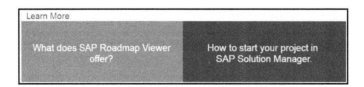

Homepage of the roadmap viewer

Accessing via SAP Jam

SAP Jam allows you to collaborate with members of your team and with people inside SAP. You can share documents, create discussions, and communicate with the whole team.

SAP methodologies space has been created to help users access SAP delivery methodology content. Space provides access to the SAP Activate methodology, as well as selected SAP internal methodologies for the delivery of premium engagements:

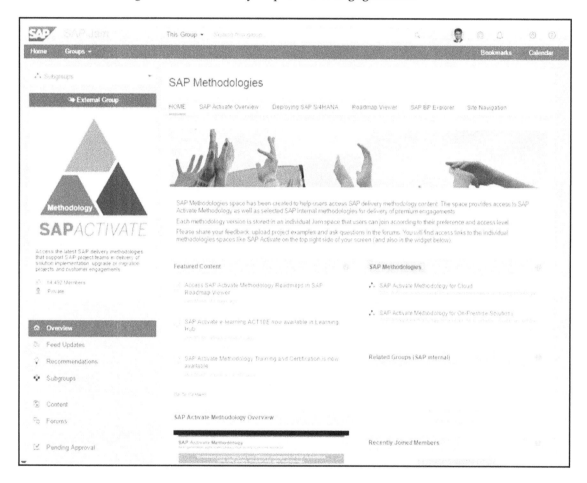

SAP Jam portal

One can choose different tabs on this Jam page to learn and explore more about the methodologies.

Summary

This chapter introduced SAP S/4HANA and its features. We took a detailed look at existing SAP methodologies, along with a comparison with SAP Activate. We also talked about the three pillars of SAP Activate and how it supports the different scenarios. We concluded the chapter with concepts of design thinking being used in SAP Activate and how we can get access to the SAP Activate content.

In Chapter 2, *SAP Activate Methodology*, we will talk about SAP Activate methodology in more detail, understanding its characteristics and structure (on cloud, on-premise, and hybrid). We will also take a look at how to handle governance, roles, and various implementation approaches.

Test yourself

1. What are the deployment options for SAP S/4HANA?
   - On-premise
   - Cloud:public and managed
   - Hybrid deployment
   - All of the above

2. What are the key facts about SAP S/4HANA?
   - Supports all data: social, text, and graph
   - New SAP Fiori UX for any device
   - No locking and parallelism
   - All of the above

3. What are the three pillars for SAP Activate?
   - SAP Activate - Best practices
   - SAP Activate - Methodology
   - SAP Activate - Guided configuration
   - SAP Activate - Roadmaps
   - None of the above

4. With what does SAP Activate help you?
   - Sample reference solution containing organizational data
   - Model company
   - Solves operation issues
   - One methodology for all
   - None of the above

5. What is true about SAP Activate methodology phases?
   - In prepare phase, the project is initiated and planned
   - In prepare phase, the customer team explores SAP solution functionalities
   - In explore phase, the customer team explores SAP solution functionalities
   - Structured testing and data migration is done in realize phase
   - Explore phase comes before prepare phase

2
SAP Activate Methodology

This chapter details the SAP Activate methodology, its main characteristics (In cloud, on-premise, and hybrid), and how it handles governance, roles, and various implementation approaches. We will take a closer look at fit/gap analysis and Delta solution design workshops. Solution validation and Model Company are also briefly discussed but these topics will be discussed in detail in the later chapters. We will conclude this chapter with a detailed discussion on the structure and phases of SAP Activate.

Main characteristics of the SAP Activate methodology - In cloud, on-premise, and hybrid

The SAP Activate methodology supports project teams in the deployment of SAP solutions to In cloud, on-premise, or hybrid environments. Customers can follow on their own, with SAP or with SAP partners.

SAP Activate has imbibed the 40 plus years of implementation experience that SAP has with its customers. The distinct among them can be jotted down as follows:

- **Start with best practices**: Use Ready-to-Run business processes
- **Cloud-ready**: Leverage the flexibility and speed of cloud
- **Validate solution**: Validate best practices with fit/gap workshop and capture data
- **Premium engagement ready**: Build and run fully supported via SAP control centers

- **Modular, scalable, and agile**: Structured project to deliver solution directly
- **Quality built-in**: Identify the risks early with a total quality approach

Let's try to dig up a little more and find out the details of each offering.

Start with best practices

Best practices is one the three pillars of SAP Activate (as discussed in Chapter 1, *Introduction to SAP S/4HANA*). Delivering best practices via SAP Activate methodology serves SAP's vision of increased value proposition and **Time to Value (TtV)** (TtV is the time between a business request and the initial delivery of that request) for customers. Customers can start fast, build smart, and run simple while continuously innovating. It also makes the onboarding of new solutions such as SAP S/4HANA simple and fast, by providing trial offerings with sample data. SAP Activate contains best practices for the S/4HANA Cloud edition as well as an on-premise edition. In SAP S/4HANA, following SAP Activate, we can take advantage of a Model Company and use it as a baseline during the fit/gap sessions to validate our requirements against it.

The Model Companies are SAP Best Practices and ready-to-use reference solutions embedded in the product (SAP S/4HANA) and shipped with a predefined master data and organizational data that allow SAP customers to jump-start the implementation. The Model Companies for SAP S/4HANA replaces the SAP Best Practices content, including the content provided with the Word template.

The Model Companies include the business process documentation (for example, business process definition, solution documentation, configuration blocks, and process diagrams) for the SAP S/4HANA implementation that is provided via the SAP Activate content integrated with SAP Solution Manager 7.2. The SAP Model Companies can be adjusted to the customer needs via configuration activities.

SAP provides two types of configuration activities:

- **The user-guided configuration**: This configuration is used to configure the chosen SAP Best Practices to add and adapt some "uncritical" settings, for example, the value of a PO approval. This kind of change does not change the actual business processes.

- **The expert configuration**: To adopt SAP Model Companies and to add additional customer-specific processes. The SAP Model Companies are prerequisites for fast and agile implementation. They allow you to start the project immediately and build the solution quickly as long as you stay close to the SAP standard solution. Model Companies are the ultimate form of standardization for a specific line of business or industry solution.

- **Cloud-ready**
  For non-S/4Hana solutions (as of now), SAP provides systems and content on demand and Ready-to-Run as per the project need. These contents are delivered as preassembled packages to enable the customer to:
  - Jumpstart projects with redeployed, preassembled, and pretested templates from SAP
  - Accelerate development by eliminating common and manual configurations
  - Defer the decision on choosing the final infrastructure (cloud or premise) and initiate work in the SAP-hosted cloud
  - Adopt a solution to project needs using common organizational structures, preloaded data, content enhancement, and more

With these preassembled packages, the customer leverages accelerated development and implementation, reduces time to value, can be agile and achieve faster innovation. As discussed in the last section about a Model Company via SAP Activate, you get a flexible deployment option of the preassembled Model Company (In cloud or on-premise).

A customer can choose from the following Model Companies:

- A clean slate Model Company
- A qualified Model Company:

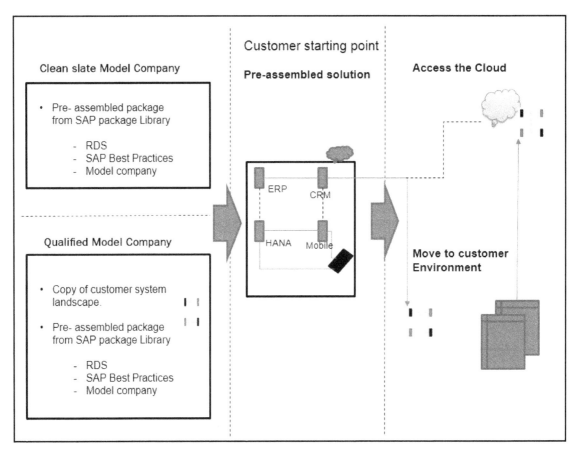

Model Company

The service building blocks of an SAP Model Company are as follows:

- **Best practices**: Methodologies and step-by-step approaches combining knowledge of customer projects.
- **Preconfigured end-to-end processes**: End-to-end processes tailored to your industry and line of business with preconfigured steps for operating the business with SAP software.

- **SAP Solution Manager documentation**: Business process documentation ready to use for discovery and fit/gap analysis.
- **Industry references architecture**: Aligned with reference architecture for a domain.
- **Engineered services**: Accelerators for adoption and onboarding.
- **Sample data**: Sample transactional and master data for demo purpose.
- **SAP software**: SAP S/4HANA, SAP success factors, and other industry solutions.
- **Validate solution**: Validate to best practices with fit/gap workshop and capture data.

  In the explore phase of the SAP Activate methodology, a solution validation workshop is encouraged to verify that the solution scenarios meet the business needs, and at the same time, backlogs are captured and Delta design can be done accordingly. This gives accelerated time to value through content reuse and focus on differentiating capabilities.

- **Premium engagement ready**: Build and run fully supported via SAP control centers. Customers with SAP MaxAttention and SAP Active embedded agreements will find assistance for the use of control centers and other related services in the SAP Activate methodology.

  The following diagram shows the engagement type at various phases of the SAP Activate methodology. Each phase is well connected via SAP support to keep innovating and at the same time making sure that operations are not affected:

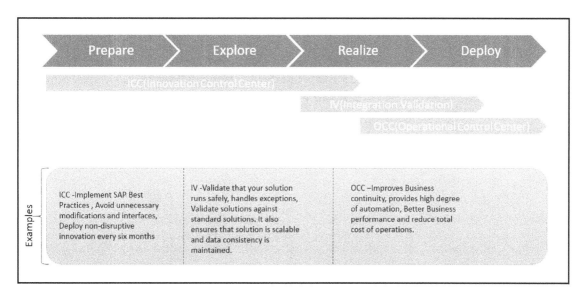

Engagement at various phases of SAP Activate

- **Modular, scalable, and agile**: With SAP Activate, the projects are structured to deliver solutions directly. It is an agile implementation methodology that will help the customer to adapt quickly to the rapid development cycle. To facilitate customer co-innovation, the whole approach has been modularized, with the full support for initial deployment and continuous business innovation. The methodology is highly scalable and supports projects with vivid scope and complexity. Its flexible framework allows us to provide prescriptive guidance for any SAP project.
- **Quality built-in**: Identify risk early with a total quality approach. Though ASAP and SAP launch had concepts of quality gates, with SAP Activate, formal risk and quality management with a structured quality management plan and pre-defined Q-gates, are built into the project from the start.

Fit/gap analysis

The main objective of the fit/gap analysis is to identify any capture Delta business requirement and gaps, which might not have been captured in the preactivated or preassembled solution (sandbox). At the end of the analysis, it is expected that the team has finalized and gotten the approval for scope baseline to proceed into the realize phase.

This ensures that implementation meets customer's business needs and the customer's solution is aligned to SAP standard processes. It also provides an opportunity to relook and discuss the solution design, prioritized Delta requirements, and gaps. A good gap analysis reduces the need for rework during the realize phase. With fit/gap analysis, the purpose is also to validate the predefined scenarios, processes, and enhancements, and identify potential gaps between the delivered product and customer requirements. The deliverable only captures requirements for gaps. It follows an iterative approach to the existing documentation and models can be altered; changes should be marked and documented in the Solution Manager:

Fit/gap Analysis

In the case of projects deployed on cloud, this activity is called **Fit-to-Standard**. Here, the focus is to make sure that there is an ability to absorb the quarterly innovations that are provided in the cloud. For an on-premise project, we do two workshops: workshop type-A for solution validation and workshop type-B for Delta solution design. Let's take a deeper look at these workshops.

Let's do a deep dive into fit/gap analysis—on-premise. The following content is specific to on-premise as cloud does not need it.

Solution validation - Workshop type A

The purpose of this workshop is to challenge changes to SAP standard functionality and determine whether there is a real need for enhancement or change that is affecting one or more business values. The result of the workshop is the list of Delta requirements and gaps.

The approach followed here is a top-down approach, where we start with an overall solution and then drill down to processes and functional details. The sequence of activities in this workshop can be jotted down as follows:

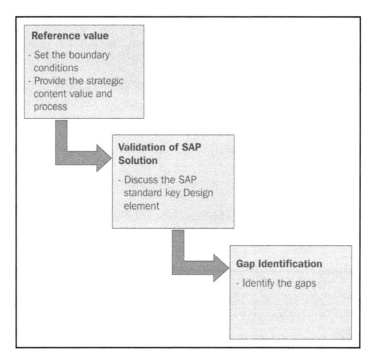

Workshop A: Sequence of activities

Once we have identified the gap and Delta requirements via workshop type A, then we can create an initial backlog with a Delta score prioritization before moving to workshop type B. Delta score prioritization is not a part of any of the two workshops, but it is a result of workshop A and input for workshop B. The business users prioritize the backlog depending on the sequence of features to be implemented. This will be used by the project team for the Delta design workshop and gives clarity on what they should focus on.

At the end of backlog prioritization, the Delta requirements and gaps are identified, ownership is decided, and associated SAP business processes are identified:

	Story	Estimate(Days)	Priority
Initial Product Backlog for success Factor System			
Must	As a user, I want to enter my work hours so I can make	5	1
	As an administrator, I want to approve timesheets so	4	2
	As a user, I want to log in to the system so I can perform payroll functions	4	3
Should	As a user, I want to log off of the system so no one can enter erroneous information in my	4	4
	As an administrator, I want to run consolidated payroll reports so I can provide a weekly	10	5
	As an administrator, I want the ability to create new accounts so we can add employees after	7	6
	As a user, I want the ability to edit my timesheet so I can correct any	5	7
Would	As an administrator, I want the ability to set automated reminders so employees will verify and sign their	9	8
	As an administrator, I want the ability to archive timesheets so the organization can file them for audit and tax	15	9

An example of initial product backlog

For premium engagement projects, SAP's **Innovation Control Center (ICC)** enables the project team to validate integration projects and prepare for smooth operations, enabling agile and continuous deployment of changes to the customer system. Project teams can submit gaps to the MCC for validation using transaction SMFG.

Delta design solution - Workshop type B

From workshop A, the team has realized that some gaps and Delta requirements exist in the project; they use workshop B to achieve the same results. Functional and key users play an important role in the design and acceptance of the Delta solution design. SAP Solution Manager is used as a toolset for solution documentation. To gain business acceptance, the methodology recommends the use of Road Show. Here, the approach is bottom-up; we go to the details and try to resolve it:

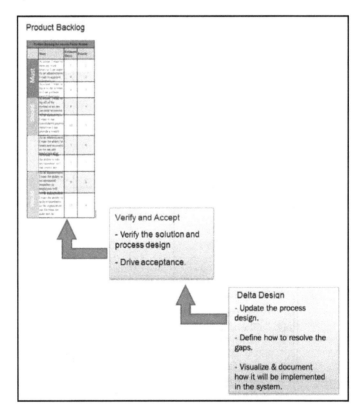

Delta design solution -Workshop B

Just to bring to the attention of ASAP methodology users: **Verify and Accept** are not formal blueprint signs; here, it is more about backlog verification and acceptance. After both the workshops are complete in the explore phase, the project team uses this information to conduct release and sprint planning for the realize phase of SAP Activate.

The following are the points to consider before the workshops for fit/gap analysis:

- Set up a reference system (sandbox system) based on SAP Best Practices, RDS, and other references available from SAP.
- Bring real business data into the sandbox system to materialize gap analysis accurately
- Refer to `https://cal.sap.com/` and other such application libraries to leverage the prebuild solutions from SAP
- The reference system might not have all the configurations required for the workshop; extending and deploying an additional scenario will help conduct the workshop more effectively
- Discuss and prepare the release and sprint plan for the realize phase.

The SAP cloud solutions are standard solutions preconfigured with SAP Best Practices. The Fit-to-Standard process includes identifying any gaps, as well as cataloging and assigning initial importance and complexity to them:

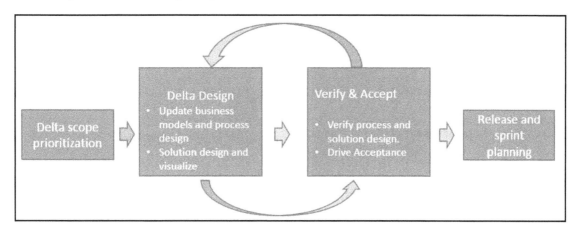

Gap identification/Delta design

Note that the prioritization, detailed analysis, and Delta design for closing the gaps are typically not included in a cloud engineered service and may require a modification of the scope and timeline of the implementation. Check the scope in the contract for it.

Let's look at a validate solution example and look at the steps in the journey from the **Explore-Realize-Deploy** phase:

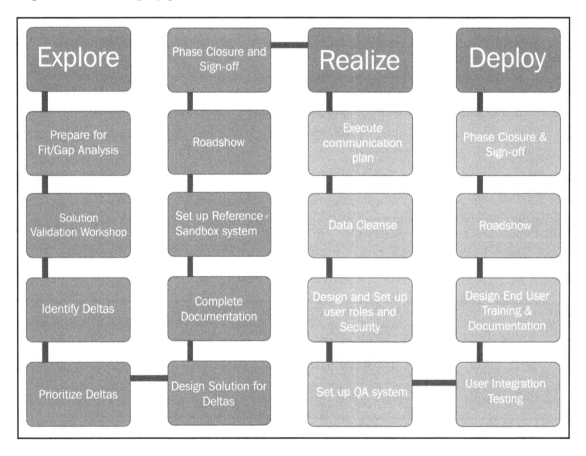

Journey from explore to deploy

The following is a summary of the deliverables from workshop A (validate solution). Workshop A starts with meeting with the customer to introduce their business and a detailed workshop plan and preparation. The first demo solution workshop is conducted to validate the process and role, followed by a second solution demo to define gaps and validate process steps. This flow results into:

- A gap list or an updated backlog as a deliverable from workshop A
- An update of the process diagrams by the customer, aligning what has been discussed during workshop
- Decisions, assumptions, and business impacts are well defined and documented

During the preparation for the fit/gap workshop step of workshop A, a **statement of work** (**SOW**) is created and stored in the project repository. During solution validation, a process map, business process hierarchy, business process scenario, and scope item process flow are uploaded to the SAP Solution Manager. While the identified Deltas are uploaded into the Solution Manager, key decisions are stored in the project repository.

Key components of workshop B (Delta design)

Workshop B is for the Delta design of functional gaps. It is designed to prioritize backlog items. It:

- Picks up from where workshop A stops, so as to leverage the process flow
- Helps to visualize the solution design for functional gaps
- Captures requirements based on feedback
- Drives early approval
- Expects iteration
- Standardizes solution design so as to minimize modification
- Brings upfront the integration challenges

 Processes such as OTC (create an order, delivery, billing, and A/R collection) and PTP (create a purchase order, receive the product, and pay the vendor) are complex in nature. One needs to plan more effectively for integration workshops.

A Delta design workshop agenda, scope item, and process flow are uploaded in the SAP Solution Manager. Also, the complete documentation of the organizational structure, business processes, functional specifications, and the WRICEF list, to name a few, are uploaded into the SAP Solution Manager.

Gap handling and documentation

The following is a template used widely for gap handling and documentation:

Gap type	Workshop A	Workshop B
Process gap	Capture requirement in a backlog template	Provide details in the business scenario design document—https://support.sap.com/content/dam/SAAP/SAP_Activate/OMP_A26.docx (loaded into the Solution Manager) and update process models in Solution Manager
All workflow		Provide details in the "FS-Workflow" template from the functional specifications zip file (https://support.sap.com/content/dam/SAAP/SAP_Activate/S4H_201.zip) and load into the Solution Manager
Reporting gap	Get it reviewed by customer	Provide details in the "FS-Reports" template from the functional specifications zip file https://support.sap.com/content/dam/SAAP/SAP_Activate/S4H_201.zip and load into the Solution Manager
All non-standard modification		Provide details in the "FS-Interfaces" template from the functional specifications zip file https://support.sap.com/content/dam/SAAP/SAP_Activate/S4H_201.zip and load into SM
Data migration and conversion	Create corresponding business requirements in the SAP Solution Manager and attach all the documentation	Provide details in the "FS-Conversions" template from the functional specifications zip file https://support.sap.com/content/dam/SAAP/SAP_Activate/S4H_201.zip and load into SM
Any enhancement to software		Provide details in the "FS-Enhancements" template from the functional specifications zip file https://support.sap.com/content/dam/SAAP/SAP_Activate/S4H_201.zip and load into SM
Forms		Provide details in the "FS-Print Forms" template from the functional specifications zip file https://support.sap.com/content/dam/SAAP/SAP_Activate/S4H_201.zip and load into SM
Organizational structure not included in best practices		Enhance best practices documentation with customer-specific organizational structure
Changes to standard predefined authorization roles or new business roles		Define business user role document and create role authorization matrix and use the template from https://support.sap.com/content/dam/SAAP/SAP_Activate/BB_97.docx

Structure and phases of SAP Activate

The SAP Activate methodology is structured into phases, workstreams, deliverables, and tasks.

As depicted in the following diagram, the structure elements are:

- Phase
- Workstream
- Deliverable
- Task:

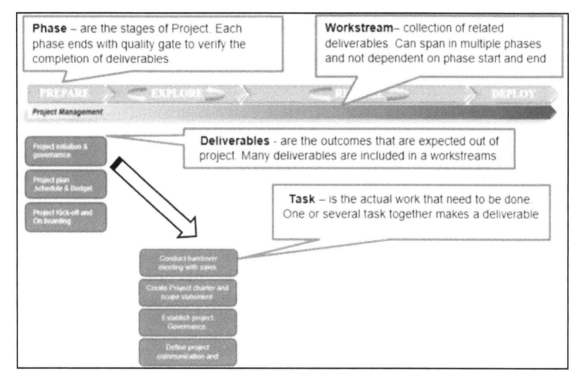

The structure element of SAP Activate

In addition to these elements, the SAP Activate methodology contains a workstream that is assigned as an attribute to tasks and deliverables:

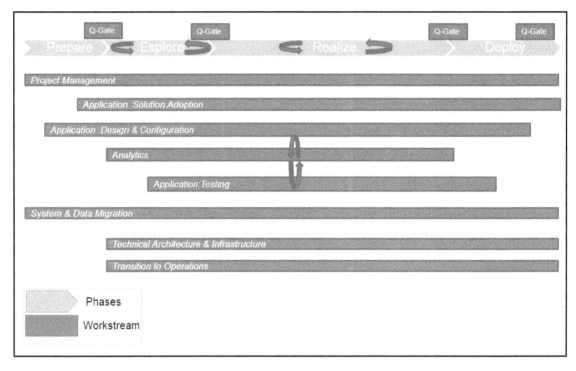

Preview (workstream for on-premise solution)

Let's discuss each structure individually and find out how they work together. We start with the phases of SAP Activate in an on-premise project.

The SAP Activate content is time-wise structured into phases. The phases provide support throughout the project life cycle. Each phase has a series of value delivery and relevant checks to make sure that the solution delivers as per the expectation. The project phases of SAP Activate for on-premise are **Prepare**, **Explore**, **Realize**, and **Deploy**:

Phases of SAP Activate for on-premise

Discover and run are two additional phases often referred to. The core delivery of the project happens between the prepare and deploy phase:

Let's try to explore in detail all the six phases and see what the purpose of each phase (in general) is and what they are supposed to deliver.

The discover phase

The Discover phase allows you to experience the SAP Best Practices content and process in a trial. You can develop the strategies and plan the roadmap that you want to use during the actual implementation:

It facilitates the decision makers and implementation consultants to have a first-hand experience before going ahead with the implementation of SAP solutions. For example, one can explore SAP S/4HANA, on-premise with a 30 days trial and evaluate digitized business processes such as order-to-cash before implementing it; let's say if someone is interested in SAP trial systems for SAP S/4HANA best practices, they can visit `https://www.sap.com/cmp/oth/crm-s4hana/index.html` and experience SAP S/4HANA with trials for the In cloud and on-premise editions. They can choose from the following options:

- 14 days trial for the SAP S/4HANA cloud, discovering the value of simplicity across concrete roles and predefined scenarios in finance, project management, and marketing.
- 30 days trial for SAP S/4HANA, experiencing the value of instant insight across end-to-end business processes in finance, controlling, manufacturing, and service.

For SAP Best Practices content and methodology during the discover phase, you can:

- Discover and explore best practices process content via the SAP Best Practices explorer
- Discover methodology in the SAP roadmap viewer

The following are the salient features of the SAP Best Practices explorer:

- Can be easily accessed via `https://rapid.sap.com/bp/`
- Intuitive and easy navigation
- Replaces old service marketplace page for SAP Best Practices
- Powerful filter conditions for search
- Ease of accessibility—can be accessed via handheld devices
- Offers project accelerators

Let's walk through how SAP Best Practices explorer works. `https://www.sap.com/index.html` is one of the entry points to navigate to the **SAP Best Practices Explorer**. You can directly go to `https://rapid.sap.com/bp/`:

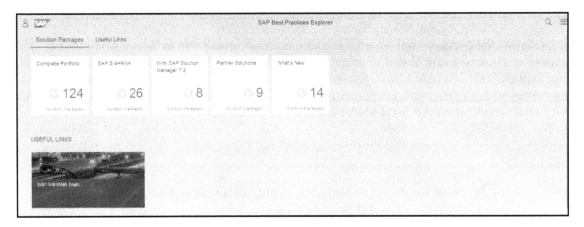

SAP Best Practices Explorer

You can make a choice (for example, here I chose **SAP Solution Manager 7.2**); you can choose all the highlighted fields in the following screenshot as a filter to find the package you need:

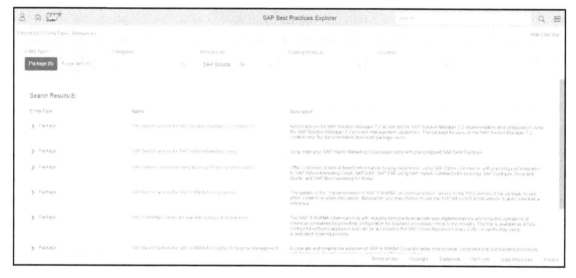

Applying search filters on SAP Best Practices explorer

SAP Best Practices content is available in the following three layers:

- **Package**: A selection of scope items that cover the scope of the next generation S/4HANA business suite/other leading industry/line of business segments. Packages are available In cloud or on-premise and can be implemented fully or partially.
- **Scope item**: Scope items are typically a pre-defined business process representing a best practices implementation choice for a customer. Each scope item has a set of accelerators and requires specific building blocks to be implemented.

- **Building block**: These are a set of configurations for a specific business content. The accelerators include the configuration content to implement the scope item(s) and project documentation for the building block.

Refer to `Chapter 1`, *Introduction to SAP S/4HANA*, for more details on SAP roadmap viewer.

The prepare phase

The Prepare phase of SAP Activate is mainly focused on planning and preparation. Here, in this phase, we define the project goal, identify the scope of the project, and create an initial project plan:

Project governance, roles and responsibilities, and management plans for running the project are also defined in this phase.

The deliverables for this phase would be the input for the next phase (explore). The system environment is set up, including best practices for Ready-to-Run processes.

For example, in the case of an SAP S/4HANA implementation, some of the key activities of this phase can be jotted down as follows:

- Defining project standards and governance framework
- Detailed project scope document
- Implementation plan and rollout strategy

The explore phase

In the explore phase, the focus is on verifying that the solution scenarios meet business needs and all backlogs are captured:

During the explore phase, SAP Best Practices content for your selected cloud solution is a part of the S/4HANA starter system.

For example, in the case of an SAP S/4HANA implementation, some of the key activities of this phase can be jotted down as:

- Conduct solution validation workshop
- Integrate to legacy system as required
- Identify and define configuration value

The realize phase

In the realize phase, the focus is on tailored solutions in short and time-boxed sprints. Build and tests are done in iterations:

For example, in the case of an SAP S/4HANA implementation, some of the key activities of this phase can be jotted down as follows:

- Configure the solution in a quality environment
- Get stockholder buy-in
- Create a cutover plan and conduct end-to-end testing of a solution
- Change management and end user training

The deploy phase

In the deploy phase, the project team prepares the system for production release and conducts the go-live:

For example, in the case of an SAP S/4HANA implementation, some of the key activities of this phase can be jotted down as:

- Execute the cutover plan
- Transition to a new system
- Close the project

The run phase

With the run phase, the goal represents the deliverables and tasks to run and operate the solution:

For example, in the case of an SAP S/4HANA implementation, some of the key activities in this phase can be jotted down as follows:

- Monitoring systems, alerting, analysis, and administration of the solution
- Small enhancements and fixes
- Optimization

The phase might have additional or product specific activities, but in general, the feel and overall goal remains the same (be it In cloud, on-premise, or hybrid).

To substantiate the preceding statement, let's have a quick look at the roadmap viewer and see **SAP Activate Methodology for Business Suite and On-Premise- Agile**:

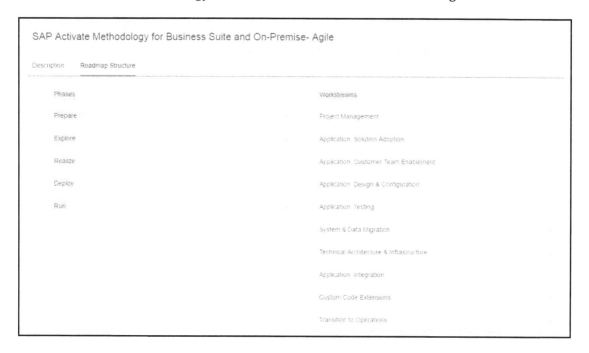

Phases and workstreams for business suite and on-premise - agile

As we can see in the preceding image, the phases and structure look the same.

This is similar for **SAP Activate Methodology for New Cloud Implementations (Public Cloud)**:

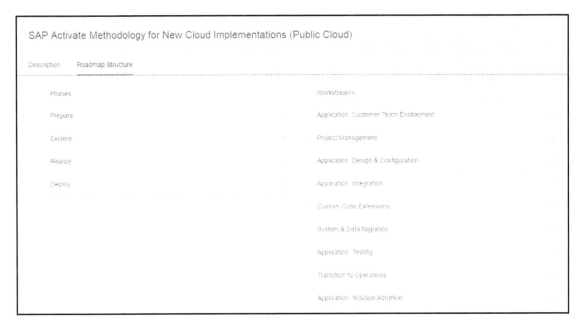

Phases and workstreams for new cloud implementations (Public Cloud)

Here too, the phases are the same and the workstream looks similar.

 Just a point of caution here would be that projects that include integration to other cloud solutions may alter the procedure.

Governance framework in SAP Activate

Governance has become a more widely used term in recent years to the point that common usage now implies a strong personal responsibility as well as a role of authority. Governance refers to a set of policies, regulations, functions, processes, procedures, and responsibilities that define the establishment, management, and control of projects, programs, and portfolios. As per PMI-PMBOK: "*Project governance provides a framework in which the project manager and sponsors can make a decision that satisfies both stakeholder needs and expectations and organizational strategic objectives or address circumstances where these may not be in alignment.*"

With project governance in place, the decision-making and escalation steps to resolve issues are easier to follow. It describes the flow of information between the project and all stakeholders. It helps the team to focus on realizing the business value, managing the risk and issues, and enforcing the standards and accountability for a project.

The governance framework itself needs to be established and adjusted to each customer, making sure that it fits the organization and stakeholder's needs.

It should:

- Realize business value
- Manage risk and issues
- Have realistic and managed scope
- Engage and maintain a high-performing team
- Enforce standards and accountability
- Align organization
- Establish KPIs and measure

Sap Activate takes these all into consideration and provides a recommendation for various project sizes.

Let's take an example from an on-premise edition to see how SAP Activate incorporates project governance and responsibilities:

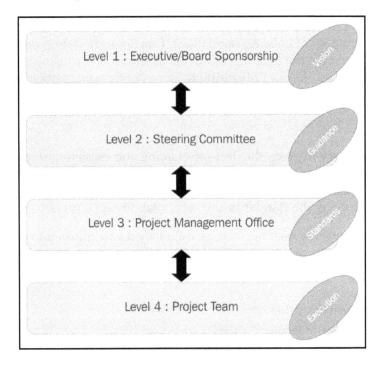

Roles and responsibilities

Level 1 has executive sponsorship who, along with a steering committee (Level 2), provides the project team with a vision and guidance. They also hold the decision rights and criteria for decisions and are responsible for the business priorities and overall strategy. The project management office at Level 3 is responsible for the delivery of a project (on time, on budget, and on value). They make sure that all the involved parties are rightly communicated. Process strategy development, IT requirements and dependencies, driving business standardization, and best practices adaptation also fall under their work area. The PM act as a bridge between stakeholders of a project and the PMO. The day-to-day execution of project activities is done by the project team at Level 4. If they identify any project issue or risk, or develop a correction, they communicate it to the PMO who in turn then reports the key issues and key risks (depending on criticality) to the steering group and executive sponsor. We will be covering agile (in SAP Activate) in detail in Chapter 4, *Understanding Agile and Scrum*.

However, let's see how a project governance looks in the case of an agile project. Here, the project teams are structured as scrum teams along with different workstreams of a project:

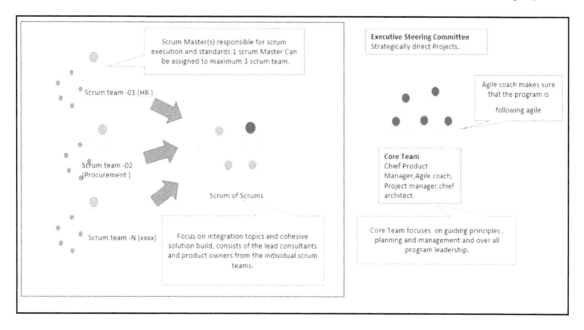

Roles and responsibility in agile context

The project team in an agile context are structured into scrum teams based on workstreams with a team member from cross-functional domains.The teams normally have members from 5 to 10 people. They are self-organized and work on the backlog items to realize the functionality. Each scrum team has a scrum master; one scrum master can be associated with three different scrum teams. The scrum master makes sure that the team follows the scrum processes and ensures cooperation between them. A scrum master is a kind of problem solver for the scrum team; he solves or escalates the problems faced by the team before they becomes a showstopper. Techniques to scale scrum up to large groups (over a dozen people), consist of dividing the groups into agile teams of 5-10. Each daily scrum within a sub-team ends by designating one member as an ambassador to participate in a weekly (typically) meeting with ambassadors from other teams, called the scrum of scrums. This is basically done to discuss cross-team topics. Teams might/might not have the services of an agile coach to help the project managers/teams and leadership team with an adaptation of an agile approach.

The team has a product owner (owning single/multiple products) responsible for user stories (or requirements). Product owners are led by the chief product owners with the structure of the team, role, and responsibility completely depending on the size of the project. It varies from project to project, and small project roles and responsibilities are often shared.

Summary

In this chapter, you learned the main characteristics of SAP Activate, such as: start with best practices, be cloud-ready, carry out solution validation, and be premium engagement ready. We explored our concept of solution validation workshops (A/B) and how they help to do a gap analysis. This will be further discussed in the later chapters and we will see how it can be used for aligning the business and customer's needs. Structures and phases in the SAP Activate methodology were also discussed in detail and we also looked at the governance aspect of SAP Activate.

In `Chapter 3`, *Use Case Scenario for SAP Activate*, we will see phase by phase the details of various use case scenarios for SAP Activate. We will go into detail how the methodology can be used for new implementation (In cloud and on-premise), system conversion, and landscape transformation.

Test yourself

1. With SAP S/4HANA guided configuration, you can:
    - Configure your solution
    - Test your processes
    - Migrate your data
    - All of the above

2. The enterprise structure of Model Company delivered with SAP S/4HANA facilitates:
    - A much easier experience of the solution
    - Access to a fully configured cloud trial system with sample data
    - The ability to skip the gap analysis
    - All of the above

3. Which of the following statement is correct?
    - For a customer with a premium engagement ready contract, additional services are available
    - The Innovation Control Center services includes gap verification and support for using content such as best practices
    - SAP Activate is a flexible methodology to fit projects of various sizes and complexity
    - All of the above

4. Which of the following is false about workstreams?
    - It is a collection of related deliverables
    - It can span over multiple phases
    - It depends on the phase start and end
    - It is assigned as an attribute to phases
    - None of the above

3
Use Case Scenario for SAP Activate

this chapter, we will learn about the application scenarios for SAP Activate and see the main deliverables of each phase of SAP Activate. We will go through the three scenarios where SAP Activate can be used (New implementation - both on Cloud and on-premise, system conversion, and landscape transformation) and learn how SAP Activate methodology guides teams for these scenarios.

SAP Activate methodology - on cloud, on-premise, and hybrid

Different stakeholders could have different reasoning for moving from their current platform to a new one. Some would be interested to do the transition to harness the cloud capabilities, others might like to use new out-of-the-box and ready to run solutions. Many of them would be motivated to use the next generation ERP business suite.

I would like to start our discussion here with a brief introduction to SAP cloud solutions and what the points of disparity are between cloud and non-cloud implementation before continuing with our SAP Activate discussion.

As we know, SAP S/4HANA offers a choice of deployment: SAP S/4HANA cloud, on-premise, or in a hybrid solution. Each customer has their own reason for using a deployment mode, as each of these has their own pros and cons. Some of the reasons for customers to go on the cloud could be:

- Fast implementation time, providing quick access to functionality
- Reduced IT efforts because both hardware and software operation and maintenance is the provider's responsibility
- Flexibility due to having a subscription, rather than licensing contracts and "pay-what-you-use" concepts
- Scalability to support changing business needs and growth

SAP offers three flavors of cloud services:

- **Public cloud**: Applications, for example, to support human resources, customer and sales management, finance or procurement, and ERP in the cloud
- **Private cloud**: HANA enterprise cloud, which is a managed cloud offering
- **Marketplace**: To scale and extend innovation (for both customers and partners)

These three areas are supported by collaboration tools and the foundation for all cloud services of SAP will be the SAP HANA cloud platform.

For SAP S/4HANA, SAP offers three editions:

- Marketing cloud
- Professional service cloud
- Enterprise management cloud

With SAP cloud solutions, SAP's endeavor is to help customers drive the digital transformation with ease. A few of the deliverables are:

- **Standardization**: The cloud model, by comparison, is more about standardization and focused scope solution
- **Seamless integration**: Native integration with the Ariba network, SAP Hybris SuccessFactor, and Fieldglass
- **Guided configuration**: For many cloud products
- **Faster Innovation**: Quarterly delivery of innovation, no long wait time
- **Dynamic Extensibility**
- **Ease of Governance**: Managed by SAP
- **Subscription Model**: Pay as you go

These deliverables make an SAP cloud implementation project different, and it needs to be understood and taken care of before starting it:

Standardization	You always start with a standard focus solution with the possibility of tailoring it to fit the customer's business needs and reduce complexity.
Roles	Customer owns many tasks of a public cloud implementation.
Project timeliness	Public cloud project is initiated immediately following contract signature, with go-live in 2 to 25 weeks.
System landscape	Typically for the public cloud solution—one test system and a production system.
Innovation	Public cloud solutions are automatically upgraded every quarter.
Handover to support	Cloud customers are handed over to SAP cloud support for long term system management.
Customer/system access	Remote—only as a service.

Table 1.1: Different Aspects of SAP cloud implementation

Let's take an example. In the case of the SAP S/4HANA cloud, we start with a starter system at the end of the prepare phase, and it is removed and replaced by the production system during the realization phase. The customer goes live with the production system; the starter system is repurposed for the production system. This is totally different from the traditional on-premise implementations where we keep the entire transport system in place and have all systems in the landscape up and running throughout the entire project and then into operations.

SAP Activate for cloud solution implementation (new)

SAP Activate methodology for cloud provides an implementation framework to support subscription-based software. It is lightweight in nature and well suited for small project teams, with the capability to integrate into large on-premise solutions to create a hybrid implementation approach. The methodology, such as for on-premise, is structured into project phases and workstreams and is powered by solution-specific accelerators.

Let's start our discussion with how SAP Activate methodology guides teams implementing solutions on the cloud (public). A point to remember when you do cloud implementation is—With cloud implementation, you work with the standardized solution. If we take an example of SAP Activate for a new implementation of SAP S/4HANA cloud edition (which is like other SAP Activate journeys), it can be summarized as shown in the following figure.

Let's quickly go through the figure before going in detail on each phase later in the section. The phases look like other SAP Activate journeys. In the prepare phase we set up and launch a project just like in on-premise. The project team does some initial solution enablement with the customer and then leaves them with materials to review as self-enablement. The initial system is started in the prepare phase to only support the "fit to standard analysis" of the explore phase. The motivation for the prepare phase is to give the project executable content to start with:

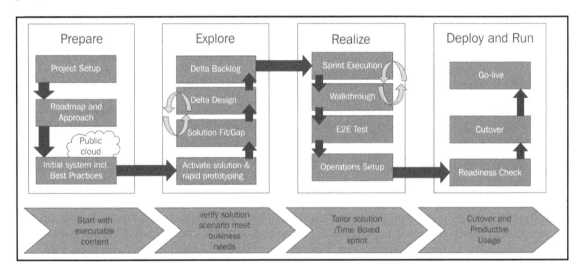

SAP Activate for new implementation (SAP cloud solutions)

As stated earlier, with cloud implementation, you work with standardized solutions, so all processes are standard system processes. We can customize and tailor, but for non-standard requirements, we would require an extension to the solution. With the explore phase we want to verify solution scenarios and make sure that they meet business needs. We use the "fit to standard analysis" approach, which is a capability available in cloud solutions. Other activities in the explore phase include setting up the configuration values, such as organizational structure and preparing the data for data load. We also use a release and sprint plan here.

In the realize phase, to start off with we configure the cloud solution using the tailoring/configuration tool. The customer is shown the configuration and is then walked through it. Different solution flavors, for example, S/4HANA and C4C, have a guided configuration tool, and both have different tools. Data migration and testing are the other activities of the realization phase. The deploy phase is to check the organizational readiness for cutover and productive usage. Many times, to do mock drill if the solution is complex, cutover simulations are performed, but for simpler ones, it's just cutover activity.

Let's dig deeper now and go into each phase in detail and see what the key deliverables are. We will not discuss the activities performed in phases, as we have already discussed them in Chapter 2, *SAP Activate Methodology*.

Prepare phase (SAP Activate for cloud solution implementation)

As discussed in Chapter 2, *SAP Activate Methodology*, in the prepare phase focus is on planning and preparation. In the prepare phase, the following major activities are carried out:

- Define project plan and goal with high-level scope
- Get the executive sponsorship
- Establish project standards, organization, and governance
- Identify and quantify business value objectives
- Validate the project objectives
- Define roles and responsibilities for the project team
- Establish project management, tracking, and reporting mechanism for value delivery

- Receive and access the cloud system
- Begin self-enablement
- Kickoff the project

Let's take an example of the SAP S/4HANA marketing cloud for our use case and see it as an example for all the phases. Key deliverables of the prepare phase of SAP Activate for cloud are:

- Sales to delivery handover
- Project initiation
- Customer team self-enablement
- Project kickoff
- Phase closure:

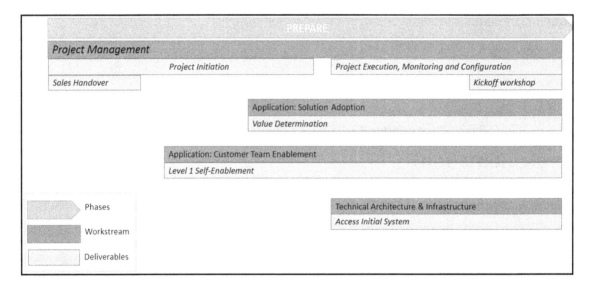

Prepare phase

In the context of our chosen case of S/4HANA marketing, cloud deliverables are:

- **Starter System Provisioning**
- **Receive Starter System**
- **Customer Team Self-enablement**
- **Project Initiation and Governance**
- **Project Kick-Off and On-Boarding**:

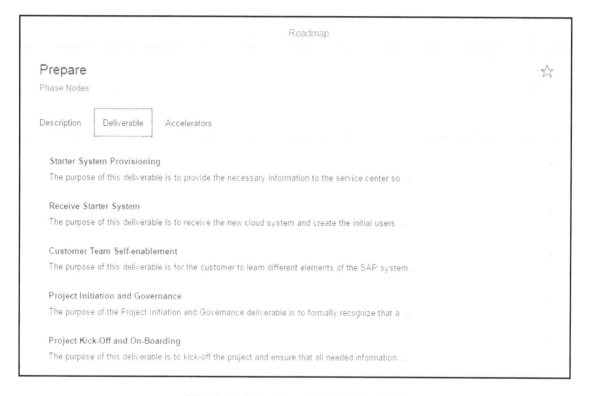

Deliverables as available on the jam portal of SAP (Roadmap viewer)*

Similarly, the **Accelerators** are very specific to the cloud product, for example, **Accelerators** for S/4HANA Marketing cloud (in roadmap viewer):

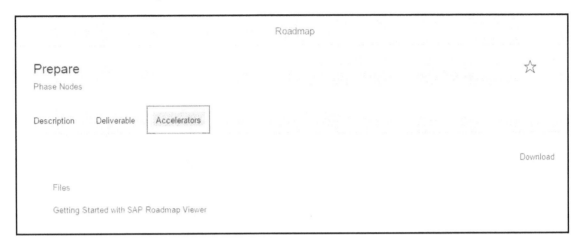

Accelerators as available on the jam portal of SAP (Roadmapviwer) *

 We depict here only once; for other phases (later) and details, please visit https://go.support.sap.com/roadmapviewer/.

Let's now go into the details of key deliverables one by one, the first one being sales to delivery handover. It is supported on the SAP HANA cloud.

Sales to delivery handover

- **Purpose**: Managing the space between sales and a delivery organization has its unique challenges. Selling is not installing. The purpose of this deliverable is to transition from the sales process to the delivery process in an easy way. This deliverable includes a review of the services contract and a meeting with the sales team to discuss the project.
- **Approach**: SAP S/4HANA cloud.
- **Deliverable(s)**: Sales to delivery management.

- **Tasks summary**:
    - Set up a meeting with the sales team
    - Review the customer's needs and the solution demonstrated
    - Discuss and answer the customer's concerns that they had during the sale process
    Finalize goals, objectives, and success matrices with the sales team

- **Accelerators**: Solution-specific accelerators are available.

The next one is Project Initiation.

Project Initiation

- **Purpose**: The project management aspect of the project, which includes the project charter, stakeholder identification, creation of the project schedule, and assigning the resource. The central document repository is set up and access to the SAP service marketplace is verified.
- **Approach**: SAP S/4HANA cloud.
- **Deliverable(s)**: Project charter, project schedule, project budget, and project management plan with governance.
- **Tasks summary**:
    - Initial contact is made with the customer to explain the implementation methodology and jointly set up the project
    - Create the project charter and identify the stakeholders
    - Verify the recipients of the cloud system URLs, initial user IDs, and passwords
    - Identify stakeholders and create the project charter
    - Create the project schedule and assign resources to schedule activities and tasks
    - Set up the document repository on SAP solution manager or the customer system or SAP JAM
    - Ensure that all the involved parties agree with the project plan
- **Accelerators**: **Work breakdown structure** (**WBS**), WBS stream view, project management plan, risk management, project setup checklist, project logistics template, issue tracking template, change request tracking template.

Cloud system provisioning

- **Purpose**: The purpose is to review the system landscape and provisioning instructions and make sure that the initial system is accessible to the project team
- **Approach**: Cloud
- **Deliverable(s)**: Starter system provisioning
- **Tasks summary**:
    - Ensure that the infrastructure meets the SAP cloud solution minimum system requirement
    - Ensure that the customer has the URL and initial logon credentials for the cloud system
    - Enable the customer on user creation
    - Creation of the key user and consultant IDs in the initial system by the customer
- **Accelerators**: Solution-specific accelerators

Project kickoff

- **Purpose**: The purpose of this deliverable is to kickoff the project and ensure that all needed information is shared with the project team resources, key stakeholders, and anybody involved in the project. The goal of the kickoff meeting is to ensure that everybody involved in the project understands the goals and objectives of the project, as well as the schedule that the project team will follow, which is one of the key ingredients for successful project execution.
- **Approach**: SAP S/4HANA cloud.
- **Deliverable(s)**: Kickoff workshop and onboard project team.
- **Tasks summary**:
    - Schedule and prepare the project kickoff workshop.
    - Conduct the kickoff workshop.
- **Accelerators**: Project kickoff template and solution-specific accelerators.

Phase closure

- **Purpose**: The purpose of this deliverable is to ensure that all required deliverables from this phase and the project are complete and accurate, and to close any outstanding issues. Customer feedback and potential references are also captured during this deliverable. Lessons learned during the phase are collected to prepare for formal phase closure.
- **Approach**: SAP S/4HANA cloud.
- **Deliverable(s)**: Phase closure.
- **Tasks summary**:
    - Perform Q-gate review and check completion of phase deliverables
    - Obtain customer sign-off
- **Accelerators**: Q-gate scorecard template and phase sign-off template.

Explore phase (SAP Activate for cloud solution implementation)

In the explore phase, experts from SAP conduct various workshops to review the best practices functionality of the SAP solution, identify the delta requirement or gaps, and finalize the configuration of the SAP cloud solution. The identified gaps and configuration values are added to the backlog for use in the next phase. A preconfigured solution with a customer specific scope is used as the starting point for this phase.

In the explore phase, the following major activities are carried out:

- Project management execution, monitoring, and controlling
- Prepare and conduct solution validation workshops
- Confirm solution fit to required business processes
- Continue with customer enablement
- Identify and define configuration values
- Review data requirements and begin data cleansing
- Prepare for integration to the legacy system as required
- Solution extension preparation
- Data load preparation
- Phase closure

Key deliverables of the explore phase of SAP Activate for cloud are as follows.

Customer team enablement

- **Purpose**: The main motivation for this deliverable are the next steps in customer enablement, with discussion and process reviews specific to the area in which the customer requires additional expertise
- **Approach**: SAP S/4HANA cloud
- **Deliverable(s)**: Level 2 enablement
- **Tasks summary**:
  - Make sure that the customer has completed the self-enablement
  - Schedule workshops based on customer feedback
  - During the workshops, lead the customer through business process best practices, configure variables and interdependencies
  - Follow up with the customer on the enablement to make sure they understand the solution
- **Accelerators**: Solution-specific accelerator (on JAM site), SAP help documentation

Fit to standard analysis

- **Purpose**: The main motivation for this deliverable is to prepare for the fit to standard analysis by downloading the SAP best practice content, reviewing the services scope contract, and reviewing the configuration possibilities
- **Approach**: SAP S/4HANA cloud
- **Deliverable(s)**: Fit to standard analysis
- **Tasks summary**:
  - Download the best practices documents
  - Review the project scope and configuration matrix for configuration items
  - Familiarize with the scope and requirements by reviewing the handover from sales information and the order form
  - Customers run the business scenarios outside the workshop on their own
  - Speed for additional understanding

- Customer evaluates the fit of the scenarios to the customer's business processes and provides feedback on both fit and configuration tasks
- **Accelerators**: Solution validation overview, solution validation workshop, sprint backlog template, solution validation workshop schedule, solution-specific accelerators in the JAM portal

Configuration definition

- **Purpose**: The main motivation is to define solution configuration values based on the standard business scenario reviews and add them to the product backlog
- **Approach**: SAP S/4HANA cloud
- **Deliverable(s)**: Configuration definition, user access, and security
- **Tasks summary**:
    - Capture the design and requirements of the organizational structure and chart of accounts
    - All pre-activation configurations must be defined to activate the Q-system
    - Provide a detailed technical and integration design of the solution to be implemented, accounting for all decisions made during the solution validation phase
    - During the solution validation scenario reviews, customer specific configuration values and settings are captured
- **Accelerators**: Sprint backlog template and solution-specific accelerators in the JAM portal

Solution extension preparation

- **Purpose**: The main motivation is to identify and define the required solution extension within the extension framework of the solution and within the service contract
- **Approach**: SAP S/4HANA cloud
- **Deliverable(s)**: Extension specification
- **Tasks summary**:
    - Create complete field definition
    - Customer specific field extensions are captured and catalogued

- **Accelerators**: Extension field specification, solution-specific accelerators in the JAM portal

Integration prerequisite confirmation

- **Purpose**: The main motivation is to make sure that systems being integrated are compatible with the cloud system
- **Approach**: SAP S/4HANA cloud
- **Deliverable(s)**: Security check, adaptation specification, and network connectivity checks
- **Tasks summary**:
    - Check and confirm the integration requirements in the test environment
    - Set up the test system (network connectivity and security)
    - Once the customer provides the data mapping and value lists along with the specification, match the fields to be integrated
- **Accelerators**: Solution-specific accelerators in the JAM portal

Data load preparation

- **Purpose**: The main motivation is to make plans and procedures to support the loading of data into the new system. During this period data cleansing is also performed.
- **Approach**: SAP S/4HANA cloud.
- **Deliverable(s)**: Data migration scope and plan, specification for migration programs.
- **Tasks summary**:
    - Based on scenario reviews, finalize the data requirement
    - Finalize the data sources and extraction and loading methods
    - Perform sata cleansing once the data to be loaded is analyzed
    - Develop the overall load plan, including sequence, expected data volumes, and expected load time
- **Accelerators**: Data load planning template, data definition, data design, and data migration plan.

Phase closure

- **Purpose**: The main purpose of phase closure and the sign-off deliverable is to ensure that the phase and the project have delivered all the required deliverables. The lesson learned is also identified to prepare for formal phase closure.
- **Approach**: SAP S/4HANA cloud.
- **Deliverable(s)**: Q-gate scorecard (updated), sign-off documentation.
- **Tasks summary**:
    - Obtain customer sign-off for phase completion
    - Conduct phase Quality Gate
- **Accelerators**: Quality Gate concept, solution-specific accelerator (JAM portal).

Realize Phase (SAP Activate for cloud solution implementation)

In the previous phase, the business scenarios and process requirements are identified. Based on this, in the realize phase, a series of iterative incremental builds and tests are conducted to create an integrated business and system environment.

During this phase, data is loaded, adoption activities are performed, and operations are planned.

Project execution, monitoring, and controlling

- **Purpose**: The main purpose of this deliverable is to execute, monitor, and control the project work as defined in the project management plan
- **Approach**: SAP S/4HANA cloud
- **Deliverable(s)**: Project management plan, risk and issue logs, and Q-gate scorecard (updated)
- **Tasks summary**:
    - Monitor and control project activity, making sure the project is progressing as planned
    - Manage project resources, issues, cost, schedule, scope, and risk
    - Communicate project status to project stakeholders
    - Conduct the Q-gate review
    - In case of agile implementation—conduct scrum meetings and sprint retrospective

- **Accelerators**: Open issue template, status template, project Quality Gate scorecard, agile scrum meeting guidelines, and change request template

The deliverables are the same as in the previous phase, with updates for the current phase.

Customer team enablement (Level 2)

- **Purpose**: The main motivation here is to complete the knowledge transfer through the support of the configuration and testing processes
- **Approach**: SAP S/4HANA cloud
- **Deliverable(s)**: Knowledge transfer
- **Tasks summary**:
  - Support the configuration process with required explanation and "how to" of the configuration process
  - Knowledge transfer to testing for resolution of defects and bug fixes
- **Accelerators**: Solution-specific accelerator (on JAM site), SAP help documentation

System configuration and solution walkthrough

- **Purpose**: The main motivation here is to configure the solution and demonstrate it to the stakeholders for feedback
- **Approach**: SAP S/4HANA cloud
- **Deliverable(s)**: Solution walkthrough, solution configuration, solution documentation, forms enablement, reports, access
- **Tasks summary**:
  - Using the explore phases (value determination), configure the system
  - Modify forms as required
  - To close the gap, make necessary adjustments in the processes
  - Set up reports
  - Get key user (customer) confirmation that the solution meets the business needs
  - Create sample data that can be used in various scenarios to demonstrate and validate solutions (or parts of it)

- **Accelerators**: Solution-specific accelerator (on JAM site), SAP help documentation

Solution extension development and deployment

- **Purpose**: The purpose of this deliverable is to develop the solution extensions identified in the explore phase and included in the scope of the project
- **Approach**: SAP S/4HANA cloud
- **Deliverable(s)**: Solution extension development and solution extension deployment on production
- **Tasks summary**:
  - Adapt the user screen as per the specification
  - Demonstrate the extension and get feedback during the walkthrough process
- **Accelerators**: Solution-specific accelerator (on JAM site)

In addition to all the preceding key deliverables in the realize phase, with SAP S/4HANA cloud solution there are some additional guided configurations that can be used in this phase (only for cloud solution). These are ready to run business processes based on the best practices that can be activated. The system configures itself during the activation. With the guided configuration customer, it can personalize the processes delivered by SAP. The guided configuration screens are a set of self-service configuration UIs, which act as a layer that simplifies the interaction between the configuration transaction, tables, and UI.

It's much easier for the key users to adjust the business configurations. It gives them flexibility and accessibility to:

- View and adapt the configuration settings of solutions, typically without affecting the business flow
- Adjust master data and organizational structure settings in an interactive mode
- Restrict the configuration activity to only a preselected scope
- Guided configuration along the deployment phase of the project

Let's take an example; go to the configuration UI:

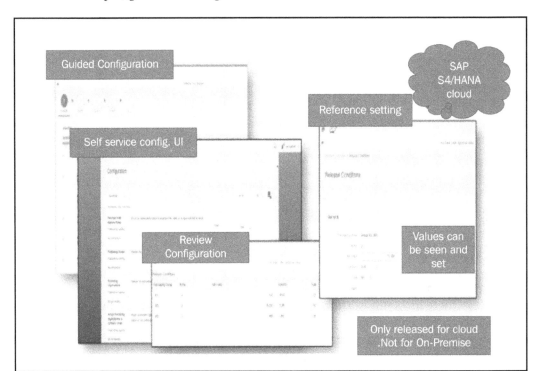

Self-service configuration UI

The preceding screenshot shows a self-service configuration UI; we go to the configuration UI. There, we review the values, adjust the values, and save them. It is dynamic and like the usage of IMG configuration tables. Of course, this configuration is limited to simpler and fewer areas when compared to IMG.

Integration setup in the test system

- **Purpose**: The purpose of this deliverable is to set up the integration in a quality assurance system so that productions, like data, can be loaded for testing. Once testing is done in the QA system, integration will be set up in the production environment.
- **Approach**: Cloud.
- **Deliverable(s)**: Integration is set up in the test/Q system and integration is set up in the production system.

- **Tasks summary**:
    - Configure integration setup on the cloud system
    - Create integration mapping and transformation
    - Configure integration setup on the system to be integrated
    - Either in cutover or here (optional), integrate initial data load into the production system
    - Once tested, repeat the setup process in the production environment
- **Accelerators**: Solution-specific accelerator (on JAM site).

Besides the key deliverable, "Integration setup in the test system," we also have, as part of guided configuration in the test system, some guided integration and setups for testing the capabilities of S/4HANA cloud solutions. These are standard, pre-delivered scripts and test plans. They form part of best practices and can be used to evaluate and review results. These scripts and test plans run in the background automatically.

It's much easier for the key users to test the business configurations with these pre-delivered scripts. It enables them to:

- Automate test runs
- Use pre-scripted, process-oriented test cases for delivered best practice scenarios
- Adapt the test scripts as per the current configuration
- Tests are independent of underlying data
- Create or change test plans (pre-delivered), run test plans, document test success
- In case of errors in the test, data can be adapted, as the tests are not dependent on underlying data

Solution test preparation and execution

- **Purpose**: The motivation of this deliverable is to simulate business activity in order to validate that the configured solution and related business processes will satisfy the business operating requirements
- **Approach**: SAP S/4HANA cloud
- **Deliverable(s)**: Solution test preparation, test plans, and solution test execution report

- **Tasks summary**:
  - Adjust the delivered test plans with customer-specific content
    Create additional test plan as per customer process requirements
    which are not covered as standard, making sure that all critical
    processes and scenarios are covered

  - Execute the test scenarios—document the results and log issues (if
    any)
  - Assign resources to the steps in the test plan and schedule them
    accordingly
  - Once tested, repeat the setup process in the production
    environment
  - Resolve the identified issues and rerun the E2E scenario
- **Accelerators**: Agile testing approach, solution-specific accelerator (on JAM site),
  testing scenario template

Data preparation and load

- **Purpose**: The purpose of this deliverable is to prepare and load data into cloud
  solutions. Typically, the customer is responsible for it.
- **Approach**: SAP S/4HANA cloud.
- **Deliverable(s)**: Data load test results, defect resolution, and data quality
  assessment.
- **Tasks summary**:
  - Extract the data and populate the load templates. The data is
    validated for adherence to requirements.
  - Data load time is recorded and may be done in iteration to fine
    tune it. This information is critical for planning the cutover to
    production.
  - Develop and test data extraction programs and reports to assure
    that the data is properly extracted.
  - Validate and evaluate the quality of data, completeness, and
    consistency in the system.
- **Accelerators**: Solution-specific accelerator (on JAM site), data load planning
  template.

End user training plan and execution

- **Purpose**: The purpose of this deliverable is to develop a high-level training plan that provides the recommended approach and corresponding activities to prepare the end users for using the new system
- **Approach**: SAP S/4HANA cloud
- **Deliverable(s)**: End user training plan, end user training, change management plan, and value audits
- **Tasks summary**:
  - Conduct learning needs analysis
  - Start end user training
  - Customer prepares completed end user training plans
  - Prepare and work on a change management plan
  - Identify the value points, baseline, and potential
- **Accelerators**: Learning room and SAP help documentation

Establish support plan

- **Purpose**: The purpose of this deliverable is to develop a high-level training plan that provides the recommended approach and corresponding activities to prepare the end users for using the new system
- **Approach**: SAP S/4HANA cloud
- **Deliverable(s)**: Technical operations and handover plan
- **Tasks summary**:
  - Assign primary resource leads in various functional areas responsible for multiplying their system and process knowledge with the user community.
  - They are also responsible for answering questions and troubleshooting problems.
  - Assign a technical lead to be responsible for communications with SAP. This person is responsible for gathering the details related to technical issues and submitting them to SAP support. They will follow the issue through resolution.
  - Expand current help desk system or processes to include the new solution. If help desk functions do not exist, a communications and documentation plan is set up.

- **Accelerators**: Solution-specific accelerator (JAM portal)

Cutover and transition plan

- **Purpose**: The purpose of this deliverable is to define and document the strategy, scope, timelines, and details for moving from an "as-is" solution to a "to-be" solution
- **Approach**: SAP S/4HANA cloud
- **Deliverable(s)**: Cutover plan and production system setup
- **Tasks summary**:
    - Cutover readiness—project team assesses what level the organization is for the cutover/transition and to what extent the support organization is operational and ready for cutover. This task also includes checking that proper governance of master data quality is defined.
    - Once the preparation is done, the project team will deliver the preliminary cutover plan task to document the strategy, scope, and timelines for moving "as-is" solutions to "to-be" solutions and for the hyper care period immediately following go-live.
    - The preliminary plan will be reviewed with the customer to validate the plan for completeness, dependencies, timing, and other constraints. At the end of the review, the project team will have an understanding of necessary adjustments to the preliminary cutover plan.
- **Accelerators**: Cutover strategy, cutover plan templates, data load planning templates

Phase closure

- **Purpose**: The main purpose of phase closure and, sign-off deliverable is to ensure that the phase and the project have delivered all the required deliverables. The lesson learned is also identified to prepare for formal phase closure.
- **Approach**: SAP S/4HANA cloud.
- **Deliverable(s)**: Q-gate scorecard (updated), sign-off documentation.

- **Tasks summary**:
  - Obtain customer sign-off for phase completion
  - Conduct phase Quality Gate
- **Accelerators**: Quality Gate concept, Quality Gate scorecard template, Quality Gate checklist, phase sign-off template, solution-specific accelerator (JAM portal).

Deploy phase (SAP Activate for cloud solution implementation)

In the deploy phase, the project team prepares the system for production release, switches to the production environment, and conducts sustainment activities post go-live. In the deploy phase, the following major activities are carried out:

- Execute the cutover plan
- Transition business operations to the new system
- Transfer from implementation support to production support
- Close the project

Key deliverables of the deploy phase of SAP Activate for cloud are:

Project execution, monitoring, and controlling

- **Purpose**: The main purpose of this deliverable is to execute, monitor, and control the project work as defined in the project management plan
- **Approach**: SAP S/4HANA cloud
- **Deliverable(s)**: Project management plan, risk and issue logs, and Q-gate scorecard (updated)
- **Tasks summary**:
  - Monitor and control project activity, making sure the project is progressing as planned
  - Manage project resources, issues, cost, schedule, scope and risk
  - Communicate project status to project stakeholders
  - Conduct the Q-gate review
  - In case of agile implementation—conduct scrum meetings and sprint retrospective

- **Accelerators**: Open issue template, status template, project Quality Gate scorecard, agile scrum meeting guidelines, and change request template

Production setup - switch to production

- **Purpose**: The purpose of this deliverable is to prepare the production system for operational use. Data load is done and its consistency with completeness is verified.
- **Approach**: SAP S/4HANA cloud.
- **Deliverable(s)**: Customer solution live in the cloud, data migration load validation, and solution accepted (sign-off).
- **Tasks summary**:
  - Request the production system
  - Execute the configuration load into the production environment per cutover plan
  - Execute the loading of production data into the production environment per the cutover plan
  - Set up access to the production system for end users
  - Verify that the data load is complete and verify quality
  - Activate the user in the system
- **Accelerators**: Cutover plan documentation and solution-specific accelerators

Handover to support

- **Purpose**: The purpose of this deliverable is to transfer from a project support environment to a production support environment
- **Approach**: SAP S/4HANA cloud
- **Deliverable(s)**: Solution handed over to operations
- **Tasks summary**:
  - Conduct the handover to support services meeting to introduce the customer to the support manager. Support task ownership of the ongoing support and monitoring of the productive cloud system.
  - Set the live system indicator in the production system. This allows support to easily identify the system as a productive system.
- **Accelerators**: Solution-specific accelerators

Project close and sign-off project deliverables

- **Purpose**: The purpose of this deliverable is to ensure that all required deliverables from this phase and the project are complete and accurate, and to close any outstanding issues. Customer feedback and potential references are also captured during this deliverable. The lesson learned during the phase is collected so as to prepare for formal phase closure.
- **Approach**: SAP S/4HANA cloud.
- **Deliverable(s)**: Q-gate scorecard (update) and sign-off documentation.
- **Tasks summary**:
  - Perform Q-Gate review and check completion of phase deliverables
  - Obtain customer sign-off
- **Accelerators**: Quality Gate concepts, Q-gate scorecard template, Quality Gate checklist, phase sign-off template, and solution-specific accelerators (JAM portal).

Let's summarize the deliverables from each phase for a new implementation of a cloud SAP solution:

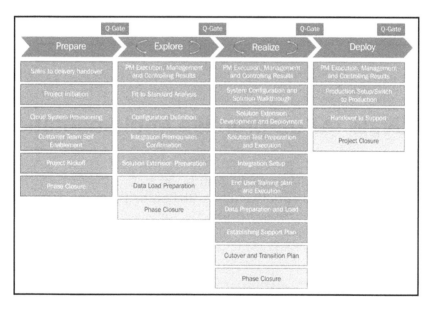

Deliverables of a new implementation of a cloud SAP solution

System landscape in the S/4HANA cloud platform

As discussed earlier, at different phases of the project we need to transition from one system to another. The following diagram provides a summary of the various phases, the system landscape involved, and major activities for the S/4HANA cloud platform:

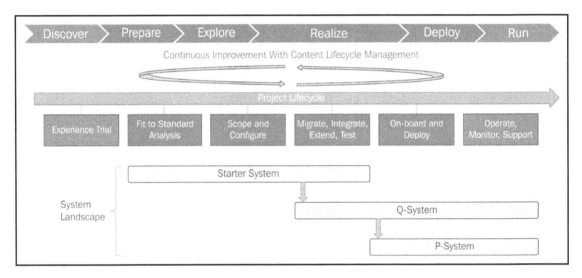

System landscape in S/4HANA cloud platform

SAP Activate for on-premise implementation (new)

As stated earlier, different customers can have different motivations to move to new environments. So, let's continue our discussion with how SAP Activate methodology guides teams implementing new solutions on-premise. The following diagram depicts the summary of flow for a new implementation of SAP S/4HANA on-premise. This is very like the new implementation of SAP S/4HANA on cloud:

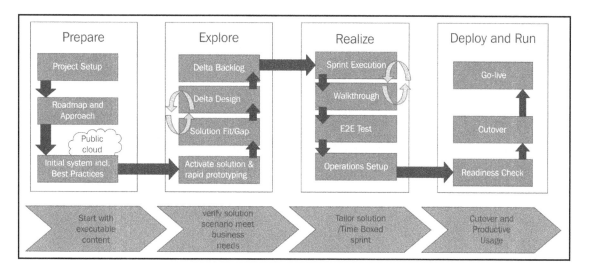

Flow for a new implementation of SAP S/4HANA on-premise

The approaches across different types of projects are in similar lines; SAP Activate aligns the phases as per deployment options. This also means that the prepare phase will differ only slightly, as we set up the initial systems that would be based on best practices, model company, or rapid deployment solutions.

The explore phase starts with activating solutions and doing rapid prototyping to create a baseline system to be ready for use in the solution fit/gap analysis. The activities could be as simple as changing the name of the organizational structure that comes pre-delivered with best practices, changing the master data, or creating some transactional data. Or they could be complicated activities, such as prototyping additional functionality that is not part of best practices, but that the customer is interested in seeing in the fit/gap analysis. Like fit to standard (on cloud), here we conduct solution fit/gap analysis where we demonstrate the solution and identify the delta requirements with the customer. At the end of the explore phase, we use the backlog list, which is used as input for the realize phase. In the realize phase, the delta backlog is run into sprints with periodic walkthrough with the key users for validation that the solution development is on the right path. This would be done in iteration, followed by end to end testing. The testing and operations steps are like in any other on-premise implementation. With the deploy phase, the technical and organizational readiness is checked before going live with the solution. Mock cutovers are performed to get all the steps right, with the right timing, before doing a final cutover and go-live. With SAP best practices the project gets a jump start; these are then validated in fit/gap analysis workshops and a backlog list of requirements is created and prioritized.

The backlog is then built and tested in an iterative manner. It is done in a series of sprints, leading to integration tests, data, operational procedures, and environments being prepared; following a readiness check, the solution cutover can be released. The project ends with a period of go-live support:

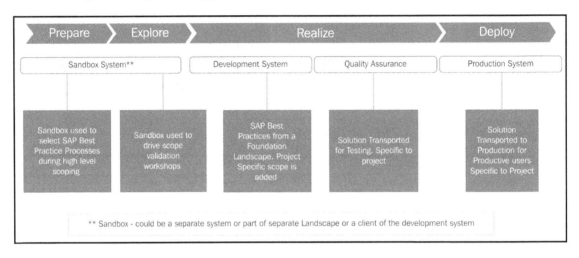

Landscape/system usages as per phases in on-premise implementation

As sandbox system is used to select SAP best practice processes during scoping, and for the on-premise implementation, we can use the **Cloud Application Library (CAL)** as reference. As the sandbox system is also used for fit/gap analysis, the scope items best practices and capabilities should be taken/recreated into the development environment via a transport management system. The sandbox system is the baseline demo system for the fit/gap analysis and is used in both the prepare and explore phases. The development system is only required from the realize phase, when we need it for building the solution in sprint execution and then testing it into the quality environment. The setup of the production environment starts at the end of the realize phase as we go into the deploy phase. The production system is used for running the productive solution to be used by end users. Aligning the specific timing of the system installation and infrastructure availability should be well planned, in sync with the overall test strategy.

The following is a preview of all of the workstream for the on-premise solution:

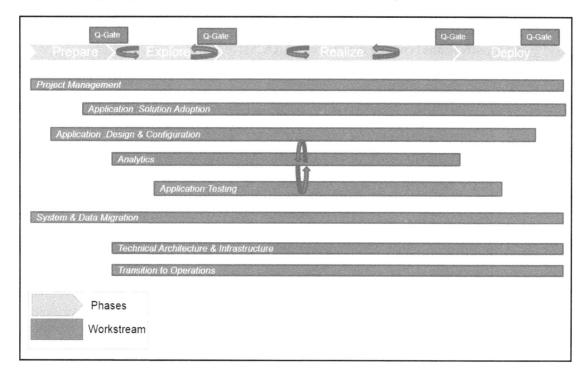

Preview (workstream for on-premise solution)

Let's dig deeper now and go into each phase in detail to see what the key deliverables are.

Prepare phase (SAP Activate for on-premise solutions - new implementation)

In prepare phase, the project is initialized and is planned at a high level via workshops. The prepare phase always ends with the first Quality Gate to ensure that proper project preparation has been done.

Key deliverables of the prepare phase of SAP Activate for on-premise solutions are:

- Enablement charter
- Prototype
- Transition planning and preparation
- Custom code cleanup and improvement

- Initialization
- Planning
- Team enablement
- **Organizational change management (OCM)**
- QG1—run Quality Gate preparation-to-explore:

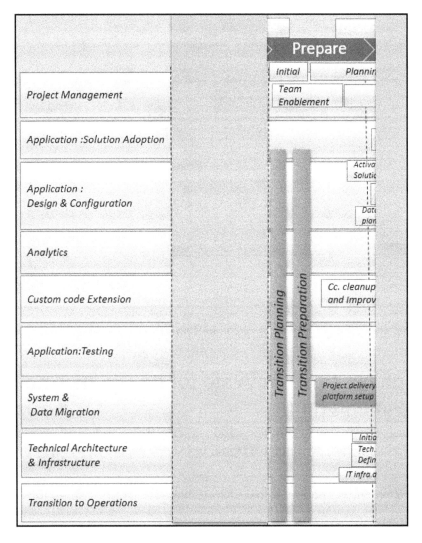

Prepare phase deliverables

Let's now go into the details of some of the key deliverables one by one.

Project start

- **Purpose**: The main purpose of this deliverable is to enable the project team to successfully and efficiently execute the project
- **Approach**: On-premise
- **Deliverable(s)**: Initialize, planning, team enablement, organizational change management, Q-gate—prepare to explore
- **Tasks summary**:
    - Project team is enabled for their roles
    - Project standards are defined
    - Q-gate is performed to complete the phase
- **Accelerators**: Project plan templates

Transition preparation

- **Purpose**: The main purpose of this deliverable is to plan and prepare the transitions in all major areas
- **Approach**: On-premise
- **Deliverable(s)**: Transition preparation
- **Tasks summary**:
    - Analyze, plan, and prepare all the items
    - Execute the item per plan
- **Accelerators**: Web pages (`https://rapid.sap.com/bp/`, `http://scn.sap.com/docs/DOC-70833`)

Transition planning

- **Purpose**: The main purpose of this deliverable is to finalize the planning and preparation of transition in all major areas
- **Approach**: On-premise
- **Deliverable(s)**: Transition planning
- **Tasks summary**:
    - Finalize the scope and objective of transition
    - The cut over plan is finalized

- Define the technical and data migration architecture
- Check and finalize the operational readiness
- **Accelerators**: Web pages (solution-specific available on SAP JAM portal)

Quality Gate - prepare to explore

- **Purpose**: The main purpose on this deliverable is to assess the items of the agreed checklist
- **Approach**: On-premise
- **Deliverable(s)**: Q-Gate (prepare to explore)
- **Tasks summary**:
    - At the beginning of the Quality Gate, the customer project manager presents the overall project status
    - Preparation call to plan the deliverables to be checked during the Quality Gate
    - The result of the Quality Gate is a signed quality checklist, which contains agreed action items for follow-up
- **Accelerators**: Q-Gate checklist approach and process, Q-Gate checklist preparation to `Explore.xlsx`

 A point to note here (in the prepare phase) is that for a new implementation of SAP business suite, you can jump start the project with pre-assembly of SAP best practices, while for SAP S/4HANA we are ready to run best practices. So, for S/4HANA there is no requirement to assemble and load SAP best practices content, as the system already contains it.

Explore phase (SAP Activate for on-premise - solution new implementation)

The purpose of this phase is to validate the solution delivered to the customer based on the standard process documentation. The various deliverables and workstreams of the explore phase ensure that the solution scenario meets business needs and the delta is captured as backlog.

The overview of deliverables per workstream can be depicted as follows:

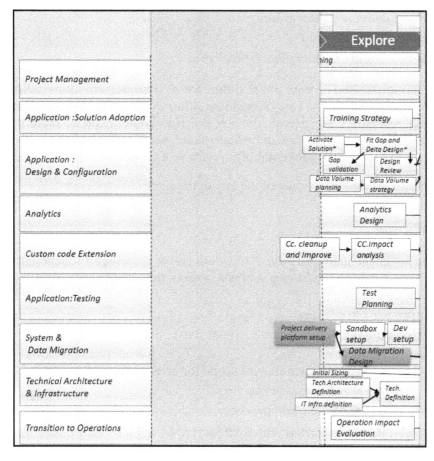

Explore phase (deliverables)

Deliverables of the explore phase of SAP Activate for the on-premise solution are:

- Enablement analysis
- Activate solution
- Fit/gap/delta design—(introduction, finalize system setup, fit/gap analysis—solution validation, gap identification, delta scope prioritization, delta design, design review, verify and accept, central finance design)
- Data volume (planning and design)
- Security design
- Analytics design
- Test planning

- Project delivery platform setup
- Sandbox system setup
- Q2-run Quality Gate explore-to-realize

Like the prepare phase, the explore phase differs for new implementations of SAP business suite and SAP S/4HANA. In the case of business suite, we have rapid prototyping, while in the case of SAP S/4HANA, we activate the best practices content and do rapid prototyping to create a baseline build. In the case of business suite, we need to download and import the best practices and then do the pre-assembly service so as to activate the best practices.

Let's now go into the details of some of the key deliverables one by one:

Activate solution

- **Purpose**: The main purpose of this deliverable is to have a functional system available during the fit/gap analysis session, to walk through solutions with the customer
- **Approach**: On-premise
- **Deliverable(s)**: Activate solution (sandbox)
- **Tasks summary**:
    - Reconfirmation of scope for activation
    - Activate best practices
    - Activate test process
- **Accelerators**: Get started with SAP S/4HANA appliance, implementing S/4HANA on-premise with SAP best practices using SAP Activate and SAP solution manager 7.2, SAP cloud appliance versus blu-ray installation, and web pages available at JAM portal

Design for gaps and deltas

- **Purpose**: The key deliverable describes how the business processes are evaluated for the fit against the SAP best practices and how the potential gaps are managed
- **Approach**: On-premise
- **Deliverable(s)**: Fit/gap delta design introduction, Fit/gap delta design finalize system setup, fit/gap delta design solution validation, fit/gap delta gap identification, fit/gap delta scope prioritization, fit/gap delta design gap validation, fit/gap delta design, fit/gap delta verify, and accept

- **Tasks summary**:
    - Validate the solution and collect the gaps in each business process with priority
    - Prepare the execution priority
    - Create the delta design plan
- **Accelerators**: Available at JAM portal

Analytics design

- **Purpose**: The key deliverable here is the analytic design, which is basically an outcome of discussion and analysis with customers.
- **Approach**: On-premise.
- **Deliverable(s)**: Analytics design.
- **Tasks summary**:
    - Fine-plan the analytics architecture.
    - If needed, SAP offers an "Analytics Design Workshop" as part of the Analytics Design service.
    - Identifies the ideal choice for data modeling in an SAP Enterprise Data Warehouse (BW/HANA), which is either SAP BW-centric, mixed or SAP HANA centric. The decision is based on the customer infrastructure.
- **Accelerators**: Road map for analytics solutions from SAP, other web page references are available at JAM portal.

Legacy data migration design and plan

- **Purpose**: The main purpose here is the outcome from the data migration workshop and the preparation of data to be used in the realize phase
- **Approach**: On-premise
- **Deliverable(s)**: Data migration design
- **Tasks summary**:
    - Migration workshop
    - Data audit
    - Prepare and present data migration scope and requirement documents
    - Data migration approach and strategy document

- Test data migration
- Define specification for data migration

- **Accelerators**: Data migration reconciliation plan, service component information-landscape transformation assessment, white paper-data quality assessment, other web page references available at JAM portal

 In the legacy data migration design and plan deliverable, the tasks may vary depending on if it is done for a new implementation or a landscape transformation. The preceding table discusses new implementation; for landscape transformation scenarios (client transfer, system merge, company code transfer, and rapid data migration to SAP S/4HANA) we would be required to run a landscape transformation assessment.

Software provisioning manager (**SWPM**) is used to install the system (S/4HANA) and **data migration server** (**DMIS**)/**migration workbench** (**MWB**) is used for the initial data load from the source system (if it's a legacy system then additional file upload techniques will be used).

Realize phase (SAP Activate for on-premise - solution new implementation)

The purpose of this phase is to build up the solution based on the scenarios and process requirements identified in the previous (explore) phase. The solution is incrementally built, based on requirement captures in backlog and is implemented in sprint plans. Once the build and test is done successfully, the solution is moved to the deploy phase.

The tasks and activities performed in the realize phase are not much different from those on the implementation of any other on-premise SAP solution. Configuration and development is done in sprints; documentation of the solution is done in SAP solution manager.

As in all the other phases, we will not go through in detail about the project management, execution, controlling, and OCM activities. Instead, we will focus on the application and solution activities. The solution build is done in sprints, so the whole idea is to get customer approval very early and bring them on board from the start. The iterative approach not only helps to keep the solution on track, but also allows us to review the prioritized requirements for the next sprint. Once the development is close to completion, in the subsequent sprint the team works on exception handling for the developed solution.

The overview of deliverables per workstream can be depicted as follows:

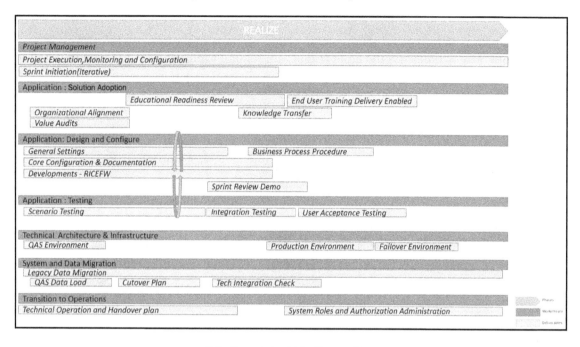

Realize phase - overview of deliverables per workstream

Key deliverables of the realize phase of SAP Activate for on-premise solution is:

- Phase initiation
- Sprint initiation (iterative)
- Project execute, monitoring, and controlling results
- Organizational alignment
- Educational readiness review
- Knowledge transfer
- End user training delivery enabled
- Legacy data migration
- Quality assurance environment—software setup, role and transport setup, and data load setup
- Sprint closing
- Production and failover environment
- Approved testing (integration and user acceptance)
- Go-live check

- Technical and handover plan
- Phase closure and sign-off phase deliverables

Since this phase is iterative and incremental in nature, most of the activity follows agile methodology. We will discuss the agile and scrum related topics of SAP Activate in detail in `Chapter 4`, *Understanding Agile and Scrum*.

The following is the typical flow of an SAP agile project:

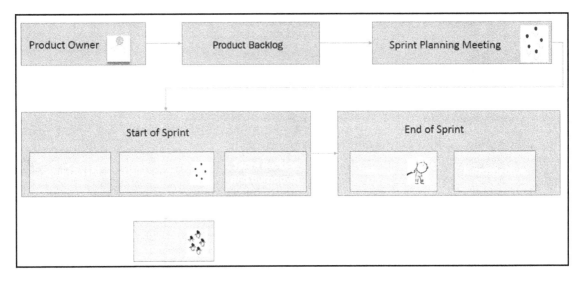

Typical flow for an SAP agile project

When we talk of agile release, it includes product backlog from the explore phase until signing off the realize phase. Once the baseline build is complete and product backlog is prioritized as per business needs in the explore phase, we will start the configuration and product enhancement in sprints for epic. This is done in iteration, and the outcome is shown to the customer. Once all epic is complete, we do the integration testing, followed by user acceptance testing. As the approaches are different in agile and waterfall methodology, one may expect fewer defects during integration testing and UAT in agile methodology as compared to waterfall, since in waterfall the build is less validated before the integration and UAT. One needs to also make sure that organization readiness is performed before sign-off.

As SAP activate follows the agile approach, the configuration and product enhancements are delivered in sprints within a wave. The sprint planning and backlog priority is discussed in detail in `Chapter 4`, *Understanding Agile and Scrum*. But just to keep in mind, the teams that build the solution collect the required information from the backlog and master files and start building those capabilities for an end to end scenario. The builds are continuously tested up to the firm-up sprint. In the firm-up sprint, to complete the delivery of an epic, unit builds are integrated and string tests are delivered. During the finalization of the sprint testing, solution documentation is also done, which is later used for operations.

Also, one thing to take note of for realize phase is the configuration of an on-premise solution will be using the traditional configuration tasks of the implementation guide (IMG). The IMG can be directly used or used via SAP solution manager. The configuration of an on-premise solution is different to that of a cloud solution.

Let's now go into detail on some of the key deliverables of the realize phase one by one.

Data aging configuration

- **Purpose**: The main purpose of this deliverable is to manage data and enable a data aging process. This helps to manage large amounts of data with ease.
- **Approach**: On-premise.
- **Deliverable(s)**: Cleanup, data aging configuration.
- **Tasks summary**:
    - Clean up data
    - Configure data aging
    - Test execution of data aging

Configuration and product enhancement

- **Purpose**: The main purpose of this deliverable is to define and document the how to move from an "as-is" solution to a "to-be" solution (scope, strategy, and time). It also delivers activities around hyper care immediately after go-live.
- **Approach**: On-premise.
- **Deliverable(s)**: Configuration-introduction, configuration-core finance, configuration-enhanced request to service, configuration-streamlined procure to pay, configuration-optimized order to cash, configuration-core human resource, configuration-central finance implementation, product enhancement.

- **Tasks summary**:
  - Create the **Workflows, Reports, Interfaces, Conversions Enhancements, and Forms (WRICEF)**
  - Perform delta configuration 1-n
  - Resolve any issues identified during the WRICEF object(s) test
  - Document the WRICEF object information in a technical specification and define the appropriate test case(s)
- **Accelerators**: Available at JAM portal

Analytics configuration

- **Purpose**: With this deliverable we configure a new SAP HANA based analytical solution
- **Approach**: On-premise
- **Deliverable(s)**: Analytics configuration
- **Tasks summary**:
  - Connect the source system to an SAP HANA database
  - Basic configuration of an SAP business object cloud
  - Creation and deployment of three stories used for SAP digital boardroom
  - Import data models from SAP S/4 HANA, HANA database, or BW on HANA

Cutover preparation

- **Purpose**: With this deliverable, describe how the final cutover is prepared and tested
- **Approach**: On-premise
- **Deliverable(s)**: Cutover preparation
- **Tasks summary**:
  - System setup (production)
  - In case of new implementation—create cutover plan

Deploy phase (SAP Activate for on-premise - solution new implementation)

The purpose of this phase is to set up the production system, check and confirm customer organization readiness, and finally, move business operation from an "as-is" to a "to-be" system. One of the major activities of this phase is establishing an operation control center or an extra care center of excellence for support.

The on-premise deploy phase is like what we have seen in the cloud deploy phase. Therefore, we will see similar activities, with a few differences related to deployment strategy. These will be transitioning into a new environment that the customer manages and takes ownership of. As in all the other phases, we will not go through in detail about the project management, execution, controlling, and OCM activities. Instead, we will focus on the application and solution activities.

The overview of deliverables per workstream for the deploy phase can be depicted as follows:

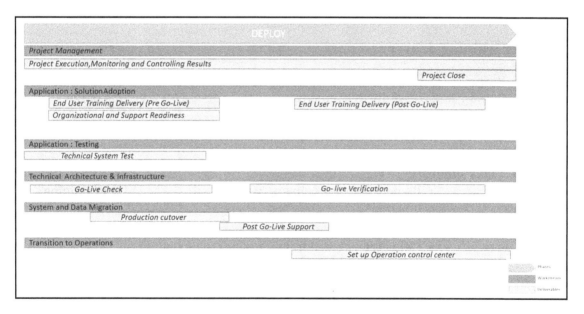

Deliverables per workstream for deploy phase

Key deliverables of the deploy phase of SAP Activate for the on-premise solution are:

- Phase initiation
- Execution, monitoring, and controlling results
- Organizational and production support readiness check
- Pre-go-live end user training delivery
- Approved technical system test
- Set up operational control center
- Production cutover
- SAP go-live check—verification session
- Production support after go-live
- Post go-live end user training
- Release closing
- Project closure and sign-off project deliverables

Let's now go into the details of some of the key deliverables of the deploy phase one by one.

End user training delivery

- **Purpose**: The main purpose of this deliverable is to ensure that the end user training is successfully delivered to support readiness for adoption of the solution
- **Approach**: On-premise
- **Deliverable(s)**: End user training delivery
- **Tasks summary**:
    - Prepare training delivery, validate and adapt end user training material
    - Finalize training execution plan
    - Deliver the agreed training as per the schedule
    - Capture the training evaluation feedback and feedback for the training material
    - Conduct people readiness assessment

The training materials used previously are prepared in the realization phase itself. Please also be reminded that the "Application: Solution Adoption" workstream will also start the end user training delivery. This is conducted and executed by the customer to enable the end users and train them before the solution goes live.

System and technical testing

- **Purpose**: The main purpose of this deliverable is to share the results and findings of technical and system tests such as backup and restore and disaster recovery, based on which recommendations are made
- **Approach**: On-premise
- **Deliverable(s)**: Approved technical system test
- **Tasks summary**:
    - System test plan created in realize phase is reviewed and updated if required
    - Finalize and execute the technical and system tests
    - Get a final sign-off by sharing the findings and recommendations from the technical and system test performed previously

The name "system and technical testing" is used as an umbrella term to include different and varied infrastructures (could be printers or other interfaces as well). Some customers could have their own way of describing technical system tests or might put them under the umbrella of operational acceptance testing. Whatever may be the name and devices, the series of tests that will be executed in the production environment should be part of test strategy and must have been agreed on with the application operation team. And we need to make sure that all of these are performed in the production environment before we go-live, as part of "ready to go-live". Also, to add, the execution of the user acceptance test and system performance test can be planned in the deploy phase instead of the realize phase. Whatever the strategy may be, it should be clearly communicated and ensured very early in the project which environment will be used, what testing, and when it will be performed.

Dress rehearsal (cutover)

- **Purpose**: The main purpose of this deliverable is to mock up the cutover procedure by executing an end to end solution. It should include everything that is planned to go-live, even a late bug fix or a correction that was done last minute.
- **Approach**: On-premise.
- **Deliverable(s)**: Dress rehearsal.
- **Tasks summary**:
    - Test plan created in realization phase is reviewed and updated if required
    - Prepare and execute the planned and scheduled test (which are supposed to run in production as well)
    - Get a final sign-off by sharing the findings and recommendations from the technical system test performed previously

Production cutover

- **Purpose**: The main purpose of this deliverable is to cut over production to the new system
- **Approach**: On-premise
- **Deliverable(s)**: Production cutover
- **Tasks summary**:
    - Execute the cutover as per the plan, including data load
    - Capture the timing of each activity and variance, if any, so as to include it in the lesson learned for reference in other projects
    - Update the task owners and support colleagues, so as to be prepared for any upcoming issues
    - Regular status updates to stakeholders
    - Get system sign-off

Handover to support

- **Purpose**: The main purpose of this deliverable is to handover the open tasks to the support team
- **Approach**: On-premise
- **Deliverable(s)**: Hyper care support, handover to support organization
- **Tasks summary**:
    - Analysis of workload
    - Sizing verification
    - Fix and close open issues
    - Handover operations responsibility

Hyper care support—in most projects, in the initial few days of support post go-live, the project team will be there to resolve and close any issues not covered by the core application support team. The hyper care support team will also undertake some workload analysis to make sure that the solution is used correctly.

Project closing

- **Purpose**: The main purpose of this deliverable is to handover the open tasks to the support team
- **Approach**: On-premise
- **Deliverable(s)**: Closing
- **Tasks summary**:
    - Finalize project closeout
    - Get the sign-off for the project closure

SAP Activate for system conversion to SAP S/4HANA

SAP Activate methodology can also be used by those customers who would like to convert an existing SAP ERP application to SAP S/4HANA, including business data and configuration on an on-premise edition.

In the following diagram, each box represents an activity that we need to execute as part of a workstream under a phase. To support the project planning, the road map links to a project file template that has a structure like the structure of the road map. However, we can model the activity and task levels differently and with a higher level of detail. The **Transition to SAP S/4HANA** implementation road map is a superset of activities covering all three implementation scenarios:

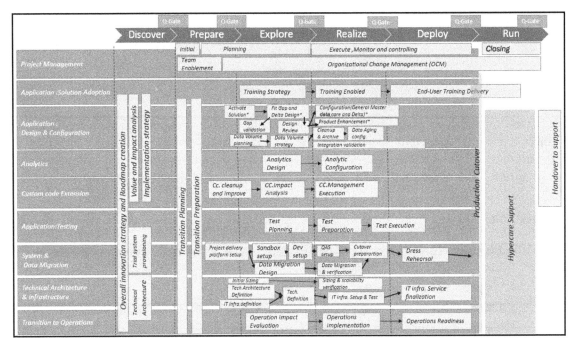

Workstream SAP S/4HANA on-premise system conversion*

 The SAP Activate methodology for a system conversion has the same phase name, workstream, and phase-deliverable-task structure, but there are certain activities and deliverables that are very different.

The template therefore serves as a starting point for project planning; we need to customize and maintain it continuously as part of the project planning and execution activities. To start with, at the beginning, we should remove all activities from the template that are not related to our specific implementation scenario.

Migrating an SAP database and application environment, along with the associated system software and unbundled products, is one of the most demanding tasks for any project manager. SAP with tools such as software update manager and database migration option facilitates rapid database migration, thereby helping customers to migrate without reimplementation, with no disruption for existing business processes, and re-evaluation of customization and process flow. Since SAP S/4HANA is a new product and many customers are not yet very much familiar with it, they might have a lot of non-technical doubts related to the conversion. For example, what the ideal roadmap is for S/4HANA, how different the transition to S/4HANA is from traditional SAP migration, how to calculate the project duration and efforts, and what special skill set and training is required for it, to name a few. With SAP Activate methodology these apprehensions and doubts of customers can be answered. SAP Activate methodology, helps manage risk proactively and make the transition predictable.

 Before we go into details, a point to remember is that system conversion is not available in SAP S/4HANA cloud; the it's only available on-premise. Also, for system conversion and landscape transformation, the start release may have an impact on the steps required to move to SAP S/4HANA. For system conversion, it is recommended to have a minimum start release of SAP ERP Central Component 6.0. Upgrades from older releases may be included in this change event. If you are already using SAP business suite powered by SAP HANA, you can skip the operating system and database migration parts of the road map.

Let's dig deeper now and go into each phase in detail and see what the key deliverables are.

Since system conversion is only supported on-premise, to facilitate the discover phase, SAP provides a pre-configured cloud trial system. In the discover phase the customer becomes familiar with the benefits of SAP S/4AHAN. The functional roadmap and conversion readiness is checked. Value identification and impact evaluation is also performed. The outcome of these steps is used to build a business case for system conversion. A "migration planning workshop for system conversion" is called, and the project is planned. Topics such as customer vendor integration are also discussed during the workshop.

In our discussion, we will follow the same discussion pattern; we will start with the phases and see the key deliverables.

Prepare phase (SAP Activate for system conversion to SAP S/4HANA)

The purpose of this phase is to perform the initial planning and transition planning. Since it's a conversion project so one of the major deliverables of the prepare phase would be the cleanup of customer code that is not in use, and which could be decommissioned before the conversion starts. In this phase the system readiness checks are also detailed, so that scope definition, objectives, and details of the conversion can be planned. The transition planning workshop of this phase also takes note of how to minimize the required system work downtime so as to minimally affect the running business operations.

Key deliverables of the prepare phase of SAP Activate for system conversions are as follows.

Project start

- **Purpose**: The main purpose of this deliverable is to enable the project team to successfully and efficiently execute the project
- **Approach**: On-premise
- **Deliverable(s)**: Initialization, planning, team enablement, organizational change management, Q-gate—prepare to explore
- **Tasks summary**:
    - Enable the project teams in their roles
    - Define the project standards
    - Conduct the Q-gate to prepare for the explore phase

Transition planning

- **Purpose**: The main purpose of this deliverable is to plan and prepare the transition in all the major areas
- **Approach**: On-premise
- **Deliverable(s)**: Transition planning
- **Tasks summary**:
    - Conduct the system readiness (current system)
    - Define the cutover approach
    - Evaluate operational readiness

- Evaluate custom code adaptation
- Define the analytical architecture
- Define the data migration architecture

Transition preparation

- **Purpose**: The main purpose of this deliverable is to follow up on the plans for the transition
- **Approach**: On-premise
- **Deliverable(s)**: Transition preparation
- **Tasks summary**:
  - Plan all items in detail
  - Analyze and evaluate all preparation items
  - Follow the plan and execute

Explore phase (SAP Activate for system conversion to SAP S/4HANA)

The purpose of this phase is to perform detailed planning of the technical architecture and conversion. The results from the prepare phase of assessment on custom code are used to develop a plan to adjust the custom code and also implement SAP best practices wherever applicable. The explore phase facilitates data volume management so as to lower the hardware resources. In this phase, we also identify the functional quick wins and SAP S/4HANA functionality in scope of the conversion project. We will execute a conversion of the sandbox environment in this phase. By the end of this phase, the functional and technical conversion is fully planned and is ready to be realized.

Key deliverables of the explore phase of SAP Activate for system conversions are:

- Training strategy
- Activate solution—sandbox
- Design for the gaps and delta
- Custom code analysis
- Test plan

- Legacy data migration design and plan
- Set up sandbox and DEV environment
- Initial sizing and technical design
- Operations impact evaluation

Let's see some of these in more detail.

Custom code analysis

- **Purpose**: The main purpose of this deliverable is to help customers identify the code that needs to be adjusted ("must -dos") and should be adjusted ("should-dos")
- **Approach**: On-premise
- **Deliverable(s)**: Custom code cleanup and improval and custom code impact analysis
- **Tasks summary**:
  - Create custom code worklist
  - Empowering on custom code management tools

Test strategy and plan

- **Purpose**: The purpose of this deliverable is to create a project related test framework, including the guidelines and methodology for user acceptance. In the case of agile, this deliverable has sprint validation.
- **Approach**: On-premise.
- **Deliverable(s)**: Testing strategy.
- **Tasks summary**:
  - Finalize the training material required by the end users
  - Plan and develop the end user training according to the overall project plan
  - Enable key users to develop training materials for end users
  - Define if the customer key users act as "train-the-trainers"

Q-Gate explore to realize

- **Purpose**: The purpose of this deliverable is to perform a quality check of all the deliverables of the explore phase before entering the realize phase
- **Approach**: On-premise
- **Deliverable(s)**: Q-gate
- **Tasks summary**:
    - Run Q-Gate explore to realize

Realize phase (SAP Activate for system conversion to SAP S/4HANA)

Functional and technical implementation takes place in the realize phase, the planning for which was done in the explore phase in the sprint execution approach. Systems and application are configured, tested and validated in this phase. Similarly, custom code will be adjusted, data aging will be configured, training will be prepared, and non-productive systems will be migrated to the new environment.

Key deliverables of the realize phase of SAP Activate for system conversions are:

- Enablement realization
- Configuration and product enhancements
- Data aging configuration
- Custom code management execution
- Test execution
- Cutover preparation
- Sizing and scalability verification
- Infrastructure setup and test
- Operations implementation
- Integration validation

Let's see some of these in more detail.

Custom code management execution

- **Purpose**: The purpose of this deliverable is to perform custom code adjustment in the DEV and QAS systems, and later into PRD
- **Approach**: On-premise/system conversion
- **Deliverable(s)**: Custom code management, data aging configuration
- **Tasks summary**:
    - Adopt affected custom code
    - Optimize and evaluate our custom code

Cutover preparations

- **Purpose**: The purpose of this deliverable is to describe how the final cutover is prepared and tested
- **Approach:** On-premise/system conversion
- **Deliverable(s)**: Data migration and verification, data aging configuration
- **Tasks summary**:
    - Production system setup
    - Create cutover plan

Product enhancement

- **Purpose**: The purpose of this deliverable is to do custom code development to close the gaps identified in the gap analysis in the explore phase
- **Approach**: On-premise/system conversion
- **Deliverable(s)**: Data migration and verification, data aging configuration
- **Tasks summary**:
    - Development of WRICEF objects
    - Development of user interfaces
    - Custom development

Deploy phase (SAP Activate for system conversion to SAP S/4HANA)

In the deploy phase, we finalize the readiness of SAP S/4HANA and its supporting tools and processes for production go-live by performing end user training, cutover rehearsal, testing, IT infrastructure and operations finalization, and finally, the conversion of the productive system. We start final preparation for go-live in the deploy phase, only after making sure that Quality Gate for realize to deploy has been successfully conducted.

Key deliverables of the realize phase of SAP Activate for system conversions are:

- Enablement realization
- End user training
- Dress rehearsal
- IT infrastructure finalization
- Operation readiness
- Cutover to production
- Quality Gate—deploy to run

Let's see some of them in detail.

Enablement realization

- **Purpose**: The main purpose of this deliverable is to train the end users and enable them to use the new SAP S/4HANA system
- **Approach**: On-premise/system conversion
- **Deliverable(s)**: Training execution plan
- **Tasks summary**:
    - Create training execution plan
    - Execute end user training

Production cutover

- **Purpose**: The main purpose of this deliverable is to perform the cutover to the production software and go-live
- **Approach**: On-premise/system conversion
- **Deliverable(s)**: Production S/4HANA system
- **Tasks summary**:
    - Convert productive system

Run phase (SAP Activate for system conversion to SAP S/4HANA)

Once go-live is successful at the cutover, the SAP S/4HANA system is opened for business users for productive usage. In the run phase, we handover all the tasks to the customer team and take a project closure sign-off. During the transition into operations, post go-live support is also discussed and handed over to the support team. During the post go-live support (hyper care support), the project team and the IT support operation team stabilize the system, work on optimization, fine tune operation, and resolve the outstanding issues.

Key deliverables of the realize phase of SAP Activate for system conversions are:

- Hyper care support
- Handover to support
- Closing
- Quality Gate—transition to support

Let's see some of them in detail.

Handover to support

- **Purpose**: The purpose of this deliverable is to ensure that all open tasks are handed over to the support organization
- **Approach**: On-premise/system conversion

- **Deliverable(s)**: Hyper care support, handover to support organization
- **Tasks summary**:
  - Resolve and close outstanding issues
  - Handover operations tasks
  - Perform health check and scalability
  - Verify IT infrastructure

Hyper care support

- **Purpose**: The purpose of this deliverable is to verify workload in the new productive system and improve system performance, if needed
- **Approach**: On-premise/system conversion
- **Deliverable(s)**: Workload analysis, sizing verification
- **Tasks summary**:
  - Monitor resource consumption
  - Check system scalability
  - Verification session

Project closing

- **Purpose**: The purpose of this deliverable is to ensure that all open tasks are handed over to the support organization to do the project closer
- **Approach**: On-premise/system conversion
- **Deliverable(s)**: Closing
- **Tasks summary**:
  - Finalize project closer report
  - Obtain sign-off

SAP Activate for landscape transformation

Customers who would like to consolidate their existing SAP landscape or carve out selected entities or processes as part of their move to SAP S/4HANA use the SAP landscape transformation scenario of SAP S/4HANA. A typical scenario could be the consolidation of a current regional SAP business suite software landscape into one global SAP S/4HANA:

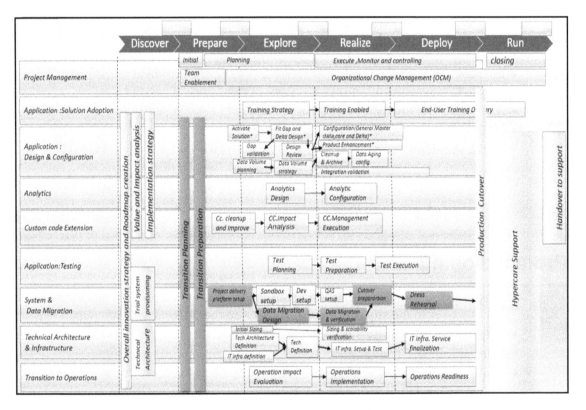

Landscape transformation specific activity in transition to SAP S/4HANA roadmap

Whenever we discuss landscape transformation, we discuss system conversion and new implementation, so the preceding figure has landscape transformation boxes (components). The landscape transformation project should not be treated as only an IT project, as it's tightly coupled with business process optimization and efficiency. There are many path options from existing system landscapes to SAP S/4HANA, so the checks, prerequisite, and action steps to follow depend on specific circumstances (depending upon where you are and what you choose).

In general, there are three elements involved when you do transition, and these elements are:

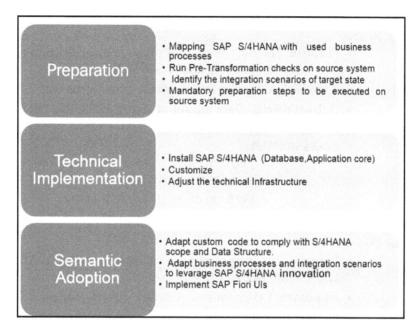

Elements for transition

There might be customer scenarios where pre-configured data migrations would be required, for example, cases with system consolidation or the migration of business units (company code), or the migration of selected applications.

Let's have a look at the key deliverables specific to landscape transformation (as they are limited, we will do all phases in one go); we will not revisit the overlapping deliverables.

Landscape transformation specific

- **Phase**: Prepare
    - **Purpose**: The purpose of this phase is to prepare a high-level assessment of the source systems and necessary data that would be required for transition from the source to SAP S/4HANA
    - **Approach**: On-premise/landscape transformation
    - **Deliverable(s)**: Transition planning, transition preparation

- **Tasks summary**:
  - Define the data migration architecture
  - Execute on follow-ups from transition planning

- **Phase:** Realize
  - **Purpose**: The purpose of this phase is the execution of the necessary steps to migrate to S/4HANA
  - **Approach**: On-premise/landscape transformation
  - **Deliverable(s)**: Data migration and verification, cutover preparation
  - **Tasks summary**:
    - Perform client transfer (move clients from one SAP system to an SAP S/4HANA system)
    - Perform company code transfer
    - Create cutover plan

- **Phase**: Deploy
  - **Purpose**: The purpose of this phase is to perform a dress rehearsal and, on success, execute the production cutover
  - **Approach**: On-premise/landscape transformation
  - **Deliverable(s)**: Dress rehearsal, production cutover
  - **Tasks summary**:
    - Perform dress rehearsal
    - Execute production cutover

Summary

In this chapter, we learned the main characteristics of SAP Activate and looked at the main deliverables of each phase of SAP Activate. We went through the three scenarios where SAP Activate can be used (new implementation, system conversion, and landscape transformation) and learned how SAP Activate methodology guides teams for these scenarios.

In Chapter 4, *Understanding Agile and Scrum*, we will focus on learning the basic concepts of agile and scrum and try to see how SAP Activate has been developed as a next generation agile methodology. We will also go through how to set up an agile project and how to scale it. The intention will be to not go into every detail of agile and scrum, but rather to correlate and understand SAP Activate in the context of agile.

Test yourself

1. Which of the following is/are landscape transformation specific task(s)?
    - Client copy
    - Run a landscape transformation assessment
    - Install software update manager
    - Create a business partner

2. SAP supports the following tools for rapid database migration:
    - SAINT
    - Software update manager (SUM)
    - Software provisioning manager (SWMP)
    - Database migration option (DMO)

3. The system conversion of an SAP ERP 6.0 EHP 4 to SAP S/4HANA is supported on:
    - SAP S/4HANA cloud
    - SAP on-premise
    - Amazon web services (AWS)
    - Hybrid environment

4. Customers who want to change their current system into an SAP S/4HANA system in one step can do so with:
    - Migration without reimplementation
    - No disruption for existing business processes
    - Create client specific data
    - None of the above

5. What holds true for new implementations of SAP S/4HANA?
    - There is no need to assemble and load SAP best practices
    - The selected process scope is activated
    - Jump start the project with ready-to-run best practices
    - Jump start the project with pre-assembly of SAP best practices

6. What is a valid statement for the differences between a waterfall and an agile approach in the context of SAP Activate?
   - For a waterfall approach, in the prepare phase, there is no sandbox environment setup with an activated baseline solution
   - Deploy phase is the same in both the approaches
   - Agile is iterative and has string testing, while waterfall does not
   - None of the above

7. Which of the following statements is true?
   - Configuration of an on-premise solution is different to that of a cloud solution
   - WBS structure is phase -> deliverable -> task in SAP Activate as well as in ASAP 8.0
   - SAP Activate methodology is designed to succeed all variants of ASAP 8 methodology
   - Phase names in SAP Activate and ASAP are the same and have the same core phases

4

Understanding Agile and Scrum

In this chapter, we focus on learning the basic concepts of agile and scrum and try to see how SAP Activate has been developed as a next generation agile methodology. The discussion is more focused on the context of agile and scrum concepts in SAP Activate. We also go through how to set up an agile project and how to scale it. The intention is not to go into details about agile and scrum, but rather to correlate and understand SAP Activate in the context of agile.

Revisiting the basic concepts of agile and scrum

Agile software development is based on an incremental, iterative approach. Instead of detailed planning at the beginning of the project, agile methodologies allow a change in requirements over time and encourage constant feedback from the end users. Cross-functional teams work on iterations of a product over a period, and this work is organized into a backlog that is prioritized based on business or customer value. The goal of each iteration is to produce a working product. While the waterfall method is highly logical, it has low process efficiency. Agile development is of short iteration with a development cycle of one to four weeks and follows incremental releases. With agile, the idea is to do a little bit of everything in every cycle (plan, test, design, and build), followed by customer feedback. Agile refers to any process that aligns with the concepts of the agile manifesto.

Agile does not mean no design, no planning, or work only on small projects:

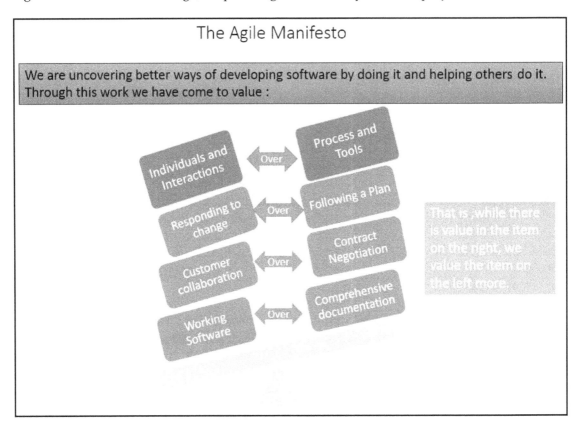

Agile manifesto

Some of the advantages of the agile methodology are:

- **Change is embraced**: With shorter planning cycles, it's easy to accommodate and accept changes at any time during the project. There is always an opportunity to refine and reprioritize the backlog, letting teams introduce changes to the project in a matter of weeks.
- **Strong team interaction and collaboration**: Agile highlights the importance of frequent communication and team interaction. At one site, teams work together and people can take responsibility and own parts of the project.
- **Continuous improvement**: Agile projects encourage feedback from users and team members throughout the whole project, so lessons learned are used to improve future iterations. This is not typically the case in waterfall and other methods that complete the whole project and then look at the lessons learned.

- **Early buy-in from the customer**: Customers have many opportunities to see the work being delivered, share their input, and have a real impact on the product. They can gain a sense of ownership by working so closely with the project team.
- **Quick wins and high-quality delivery**: Breaking down the project into iterations (manageable units) allows the team to focus on high-quality development, testing, and collaboration. Conducting testing during each iteration means that bugs get identified and solved more quickly. And this high-quality software can be delivered faster with consistent, successive iterations.

On the flip side, agile has some disadvantages:

- **The final product may be very different**: If the agile project was started without a definitive plan, the final product can look different to what was initially intended. Because agile is so flexible, new iterations may be added based on evolving customer feedback, which can lead to a very different final deliverable.
- **Time commitment from team members, especially the developers**: Agile is most successful when the development team is completely dedicated to the project. Active involvement and collaboration is required throughout the agile process, which is more time consuming than a traditional approach. It also means that the developers need to commit to the entire duration of the project.
- Documentation could be neglected.
- A good mix of team members is required, with deep knowledge of the topics. Lack of detailed subject knowledge/SMEs could lead to issues in the team skillset and product development.

Let's try to jot down the differences between agile and the waterfall methodology:

Waterfall methodology	Agile methodology
Development is divided into phases	Development is in sprints
Structured, often rigid	Flexible
Non-iterative in nature	Iterative
No scope to change the requirements once the project starts	Changes allowed even after the initial planning has been completed
All the project development phases, such as designing, development, testing, and so on, are completed once	Planning, development, prototyping, and other software development phases can appear more than once
Testing phase comes after the build phase	Testing is concurrently done alongside development as it works in smaller sprints

No customer engagement, treated as internal process	Customers are engaged right from the start
Sequential process with less collaborative team input	Highly collaborative and faster problem solving
Best suited for projects with clearly defined requirements and no changes expected	Best suited for projects where frequent overhauls are done

Comparative study of waterfall methodology and agile

Scrum is a lightweight process framework within which people can address complex problems. Scrum is a subset of agile and one of the most popular process frameworks for implementing agile. Scrum is a highly prescriptive framework with specific roles and ceremonies. It is an iterative software development model used to manage complex software and product development. Fixed-length iterations, called sprints, lasting one to two weeks, allows the team to ship software on a regular basis. At the end of each sprint, stakeholders and team members meet to plan the next steps:

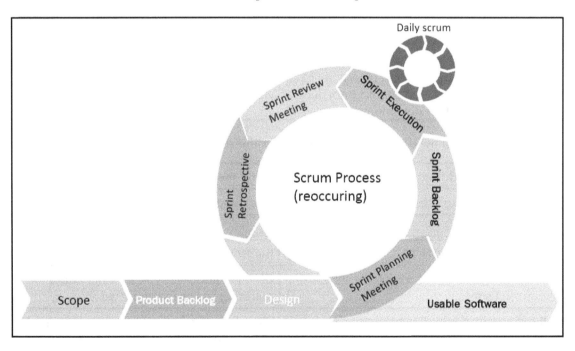

Scrum process

The three pillars of scrum are:

- Transparency
- Inspection
- Adaptation

Some of the advantages of scrum are:

- **Transparency and project visibility**: With daily stand-up meetings, there is clarity and transparency in terms of who is doing what. This avoids a lot of miscommunication and confusion. Issues are identified in advance and the team gets sufficient time to solve it.
- **Team accountability**: The team collectively decides what work they can complete in each sprint and do not have to rely on or wait for a project manager. There is more cooperation and team members help each other and empower each team member to be independent.
- **Flexibility for changes**: With constant feedback and short sprints, it's easier to accommodate changes.
- **Cost saving**: Regular communication makes sure that the team is aware of all issues and changes as soon as they arise, helping to lower expenses and increase quality.

Though scrum offers a lot of benefits, it too has some downsides:

- **Risk of scope overshoot**: With no completion date, stakeholders may be tempted to keep requesting additional functionality.
- **Team requires experience and commitment**: With defined roles and responsibilities, the team needs to be familiar with scrum principles to succeed. The team also needs to commit to the daily scrum meetings and stay on the team for the duration of the project.
- **The scrum master can make or break**: The scrum master has a very tricky role to play. He is not the project manager and so he does not have authority; if he tries to control the team, the project will fail.
- **Lack of clarity in task definition**: Project costs and the timeline will be detrimental if the task is not well defined.

SAP Activate - next generation agile methodology

SAP is positioning SAP Activate methodology as the next generation agile methodology to drive customer success. It caters to customer-specific configuration and extension requirements to reflect a customer's own business practices while remaining extremely scalable, nimble enough for smaller engagements, and more robust for larger projects. With SAP Activate, customers achieve fast and cost-effective deployment of SAP innovations with one simple, modular, and agile methodology. It is modular, flexible, and agile enough to accommodate today's and the future's delivery approaches. It enables co-innovation with customers. SAP Activate has imbibed the concept of agile in each phase of the methodology. And it clearly has the three pillars of scrum, transparency, inspection, and adaptation, on its side. Unlike the waterfall methodology, SAP Activate has an iterative build and solution validation, which helps it to fail fast (detect defects) and identify gaps much earlier, so the team gets sufficient time to fix them. The agile approach of SAP Activate is available in both the cloud as well as n-premise:

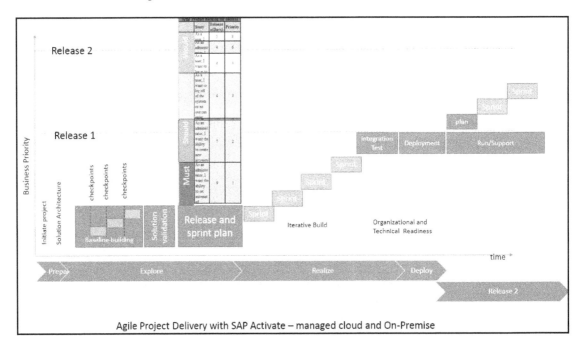

Sap Activate: Agile project delivery

The preceding figure shows the agile delivery concept of SAP Activate in phases. A separate workshop (A/B) is used to create the product backlog. The number of sprints and the duration of these varies (as it does with any agile project) from project to project.

If we take a closer look at the benefits that SAP Activate provides at each phase by imbibing the scrum concept, we can observe that within the prepare phase you can **Jump Start** with a pre-built system or preassembled solution. In the explore phase, the iterative baseline build is done, buy-in from the customer is done via solution validation (in workshop A), and gap/fit analysis helps to do the delta design. **Release planning** is also done in the explore phase, which helps to drive the priority depending on business needs and usage. In the realize phase, sprints are executed and epics are delivered. Demos are done in this phase. This phase provides the **visibility**. The following figure shows these benefits:

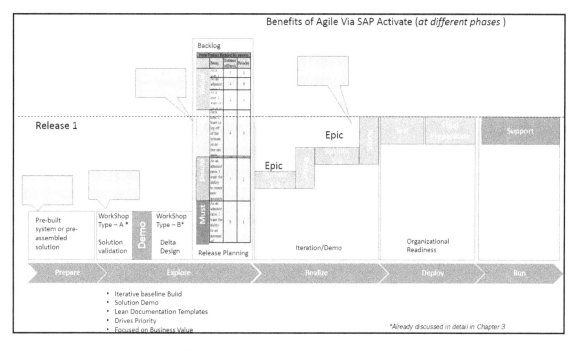

SAP Activate harnesses agile concepts at each phase of methodology

Understanding the scrum team - roles and responsibilities

The following diagram shows the framework for scrum. There are various steps in the scrum flow. Let's look at each of them one by one under different headings:

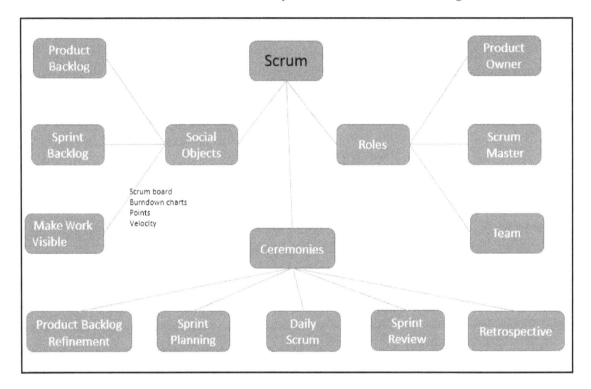

Scrum framework

- **Roles and responsibilities in scrum**: There are three specific roles in scrum:
    - **Product owner**: The scrum product owner has the vision of what he/she wants to build and conveys that vision to the team. The roles of the product owner are:
        - Defining and prioritizing the features of the product backlog
        - Deciding on the release date and content

- Responsibility for the profitability of the product (ROI)
- Accepting or rejecting work results
- Adopting changes in features and priorities at every iteration
- Removing obstacles and shielding the team from interference
- Responsibility for improving performance of the team, ensuring the team is fully functional and productive
- Attending daily stand-up meeting, iteration reviews, and planning meetings

- **Scrum master**: The scrum master is the one who helps the team to do their best possible work. His major roles and responsibilities are:
  - Organizing meetings (stand-up meetings)
  - Making sure that the team follows scrum processes
  - Dealing with roadblocks and challenges
  - Working with the product owner to ensure that the product backlog is ready for the next sprint
  - Having responsibility and authority over the process but not over the team

- **Scrum team**: The scrum team owns the plan for each sprint and they anticipate how much work they can complete in each sprint. They are:
  - Cross-functional (including testing)
  - A self-organizing/managing group of individuals with autonomy regarding how to achieve commitments
  - Typically three to nine people
  - Independent within project guidelines to do everything to reach the iteration goal

- **Meetings in scrum**: In scrum, we have different kinds of meeting. Let's look at a few of them:
    - **Product backlog**: Every scrum project is driven by a product and the vision of the product owner. The product owner and scrum team meet to prioritize the items on the product backlog (the work on the product backlog comes from user stories and requirements). The product owner expresses his vision in a product backlog, and he creates a priority list of what is required based on the value it creates for a customer or a business. The highest value item is at the top of the list. A product backlog helps the product owner keep track of all the features that stakeholders would like to include in the product. In other words, the product backlog is kind of like a wish list of all possible features in the final product. The product backlog evolves over the lifetime of the project and items are reprioritized (they can be removed as well). Anyone can add features to the product backlog, with the product owner prioritizing each one:
        - Unlike a sprint backlog, the product backlog is always changing and improving
        - Anyone can put anything on the backlog, but the product owner has the final authority
        - Most scrum teams use user stories as product backlog items
    - **Sprint planning**: Before each sprint, the product owner presents the top items on the backlog to the team in a sprint planning meeting. In the sprint planning:
        - The product owner presents a backlog to the scrum master and team
        - A spring backlog is deliverable
        - The meeting is attended by the product owner, scrum master, and the entire scrum
        - Outside stakeholders may attend by invitation of the team (but this is rare in most companies)
        - Depending on the sprint length, the sprint planning meeting could be different

A general rule of thumb is to multiply the number of weeks in our sprint by two hours to get the total sprint planning meeting length.

- **Daily scrum/stand-up**: The daily scrum is a 15 minute stand-up meeting where team members talk about their goals and any issues that have come up:
    - It is typically held in the same location and at the same time each day
    - The team self-organizes to improve performance
    - New daily plans for implementation and impediment removal are deliverable
    - It is also known as a **daily huddle** or **morning roll-call**
    - They stand up to keep the meeting short

- **Sprint review**: At the end of each sprint the:
    - Team presents a backlog that is DONE to the product owner and stakeholders.
    - Velocity are deliverable (what the product owner confirms is DONE), as well as feedback (used to update the product backlog) and potentially shippable product increments.
    - For each week of the sprint duration, apply one hour of meeting time for customer reviews.

- **Retrospective**: This is a meeting that's held at the end of an iteration, where the team reflects on what happened in the iteration and identifies actions or improvements going forward:
    - The scrum master and team identify the top process improvement (the kaizen)
    - The kaizen is put in the sprint backlog with a measurable acceptance test
    - For each week of sprint duration, apply 45 minutes of a retrospective

Other artifacts and tools used in the scrum are:

- **Scrum board**: This helps to visualize the sprint backlog. The board can have different forms; it traditionally involves index cards, post-it notes, or a whiteboard. The scrum board is usually divided into three categories: to-do, work in progress, and done. The scrum team needs to update the board throughout the entire sprint:

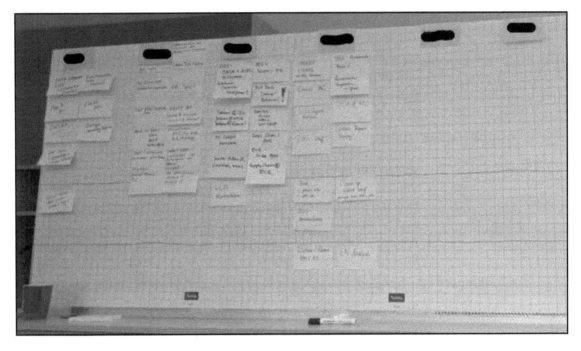

A typical scrum board

Scrum user stories

- A user story is a story told by the user specifying how the system is supposed to work, and written on a card with an estimation of how long it will take to implement.
- It sets the tone for the subsequent necessary conversation to fill in the details of what is wanted.
- The cards (as shown earlier) are used as tokens in the planning process after assessment of the business value and risk.

Widely used templates for user stories are:

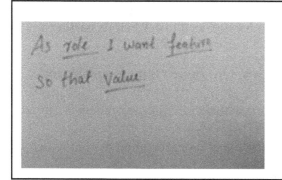 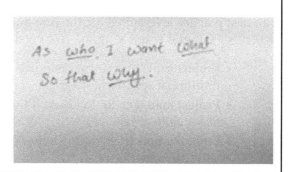

Templates used for user stories

- **Burndown chart**: A burndown chart represents all the outstanding work. The backlog is usually on the vertical axis, with time along the horizontal axis:
  - The work remaining can be represented by story points, team days, or another metrics
  - It acts as reminder as to whether things are going in the right direction or not
- **Large-scale scrum**: This is a framework that helps to extend the rules and guidelines without losing the core of the scrums when you scale the scrums to hundreds of developers.

The failure modes of a scrum are:

- No stable teams or people not assigned fully to one team
- Poor user stories, no clear definition of READY (bad product owner)
- Taking too much into a sprint and failing to deliver the working software
- Daily meetings and not replanting and removing impediments
- Not fixing bugs found inside a sprint; integration bugs
- Working on too many stories at once inside the sprint
- No clear definition of DONE
- Failure to have a plan for interruption or emergencies
- Not executing improvements identified in the retrospective
- Overburdening the team (bad management, no happiness metric)

Using agile in larger projects

Agile does not guarantee project cost reduction; rather, it is designed to jump start a project with best practice leveraging. So, the first question that we need to ask before starting a project is: "To agile or not to agile?" We need to take into consideration:

- **Project fit**: Without any prejudice, evaluate if the project is more suitable for traditional approach or agile.
- **Project manager fit**: Evaluate if the project manager in discussion here is a good fit for agile or not.
- **Organization fit**: Is the customer environment and organization ready for an agile approach?
- **Project team and stakeholder fit**: Make sure the project team members are ready to follow the scrum.

Large projects in general are not easy to implement. When we look at the scale, team composition, and organizational bureaucracy that is involved, implementing large projects using agile becomes more difficult. The approach to deal with a large project agile structure is to develop a portfolio, program, and project agile approach where responsibility and risks are managed throughout the business. Various experts have stated different pitfalls that one might face during a large agile project. Let's go through some of them and see what could be done to avoid the pitfalls:

- The scrum focuses on short (one month) sprints, but in most large projects, organizations and managers strive to plan in as much detail as possible to the end of the project. They want to identify critical paths, plan resources, and so on. Avoid doing it, it does not work. Rather, use rolling wave planning, where plans are detailed in the short-term, but get progressively more generalized and flexible in the long-term.
- As the size of the team increases and dependencies between teams get more tangled, we need to combine bottom-up (scrum-style) and top-down (traditional) planning.
- In a big project, we often hear "the customer does not want a release every month". So, it's like a catch-22, as scrum practices quick releases. The work around for this could be: "Release early and often internally, with longer cycles for expanded audiences".

- One of the common discussions about problems that large project face is that everyone cannot be trusted in large teams, and how do you handle specialized topics in such teams? Transparency becomes crucial, especially for the quality of data. Also, we should apply lean to handle topics related to specialization.

SAP projects in general are large projects and they, too, face the preceding challenges and pitfalls. Agile has been used successfully in SAP projects of various sizes and solution scopes.

Example scenarios

Let's take an example of an ERP implementation (global for a company). The company wanted to create one ERP landscape/solution on the SAP S/4HANA platform. The company operations (including systems/data) are distributed across three different regions: APJ, EMEA, and North America. Like any other big SAP project, this project had similar challenges, some of which are jotted down here:

- Due to different locations and team size, coordination for planning and execution was a nightmare
- Different regions with local product feature preferences created conflicts of interest
- There were cultural differences and higher communication demands
- The need for integration was high, be it functional or technical
- There was a higher need for the organizational adaptation of agile
- Due to different geographical locations, decision-making processes were distributed and the sign off/review process was taking a longer time than usual

To solve the preceding challenges, the experienced project and program manager decided on using SAP Activate methodology, as recommended by SAP for S/4HANA. They already had vast experience in scrum processes and had been practicing them for a long time. The project team in this project discussed and followed the industry-wide practice of starting with a small core team, which was assigned the task of setting up the structure of the project and identifying the initial product backlog. They knew that scrum would not work for such a huge team and project, so the way forward was to embrace scrum of scrum. They set up a scrum team at different levels. They had a core team that was only doing planning activities. Similarly, an expert integration team was set up for taking care of the integration needs of the project. To overcome the complexity of multiple product owners, they created a hierarchical product backlog (shown in the following figure titled scrum of scrum: backlog development).

If compared to release management terms, we could have a similar set up in the form of demand management, technical architect, CoE project team, and technical release managers. A pilot was done with only one business unit to start with. The governance setup for the project is illustrated in the figure titled: Product ownership (setting up the hierarchy).

The team followed scrum of scrum for backlog development, as shown here:

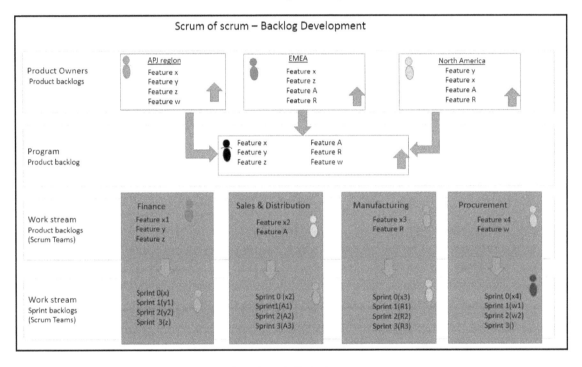

Scrum of scrum: backlog development

To solve the complexities of product ownership, it very common practice, and it was used in the preceding case as well, to establish the product ownership hierarchy to involve all key stakeholders in the right stage of the product. Product owners maximize impact. Each holds different kinds of meetings at the required intervals. For example, the chief product owner holds weekly or biweekly product owner meetings, and the project manager might be doing a daily project review. The idea of such a sync up is to coordinate and align work and discuss the cross-topic dependencies. The information is shared by the scrum masters to his/her team:

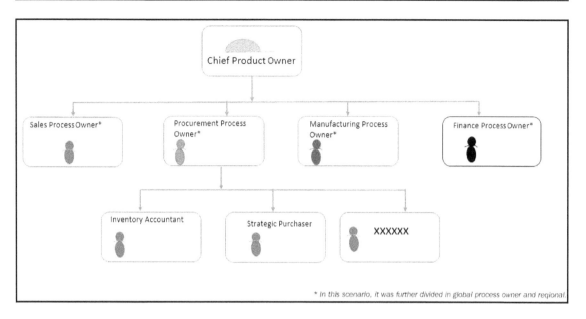

Product ownership (setting up the hierarchy)

After finalizing the product ownership complexity, it is time to do sprint planning and execution. The work stream and the product backlog was created during workshop A and B (discussed earlier) in the explore phase of SAP Activate. For the sprint planning, the team developed common themes for sprints across different work streams. Product development dependencies were evaluated and explored and the development of the product was prioritized and planned accordingly. Since it was a global team with different organizational codes, it was also ensured that the team did not miss out on common master and organizational structures. A preparation sprint, sprint zero, was added for the product backlog, release plan, and infrastructural setup. For the execution of the sprint, an integration sprint was added to integrate the functions. It was also important to work in sync with cross-functional story lines.

The following is an overview of how it was done:

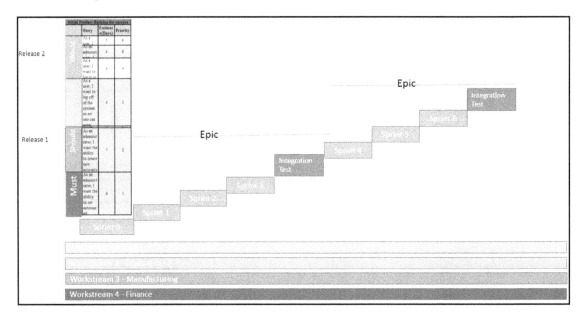

Sprint planning and execution

With big projects and scrum teams, as discussed earlier, the biggest challenge is governance. How do we handle project governance? This was one of the challenges that the project team faced.

The team followed the standard scrum governance practices and implemented the following structure for the project:

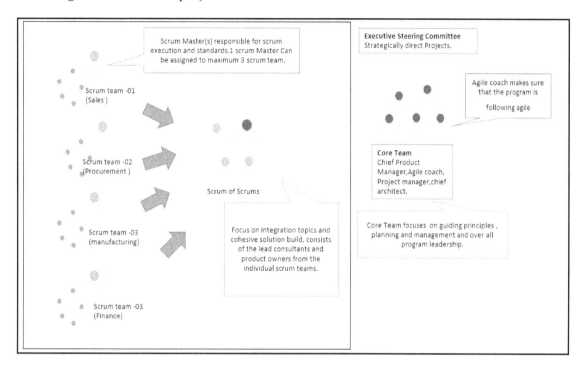

Governance setup

Summary

In this chapter, we revisited the concepts of agile and scrum. We explored the benefits and flip side of agile (scrum) and understood the agile manifesto. A comparative study was done on waterfall and agile methodologies. Emphasis was given to understanding the scrum framework and terminology related to it. We also learned how to set up an agile project and scale it.

In Chapter 5, *Sample Projects*, we will look at a sample project. We will see how the concepts of agile work in SAP projects. We will take multiple examples from various real-time projects and see how capturing and documenting user requirements, creating product backlogs (all in SAP project perspective) can be done. We will take a closer look at the various phases of SAP Activate and look at how agile concepts are used in those phases. Industry best practices are also shared during the discussion of the various concepts.

Test yourself

1. What are the three pillars of scrum?
   - Transparency, Iteration, Adaptation
   - Transparency, Inspection, Adaptation
   - Viability, Demo, Scalability
   - Fast, Repetitive, Agile

2. Scrum can be only be used for:
   - Small projects with limited team size
   - Big projects with a multi-location team
   - A project with fixed cost and fixed resources
   - None of the above

3. What is scrum of scrum?
   - A technique to scale scrum up to a large group
   - Used when team size is small
   - Only a selected member of a scrum team participates in the scrum of scrum
   - All the above

4. In the explore phase of SAP Activate, the which activities are done?
   - Solution demo and validation
   - Iterative baseline build
   - Release planning and product backlog creation
   - All the above

5. The chief product owner is:
   - Needed when scrum is scaled up
   - The single point of accountability for the complete project
   - Required to report to product owners
   - None of the above

5
Sample Projects

In this chapter, we will make our learning into sample projects using concepts that we have learned in the previous chapters. We will look at how concepts of agile work in SAP projects. We will take multiple examples from various real-time projects and see how capturing and documenting user requirements and creating product backlog (all in a SAP project perspective) can be done. We will take a closer look at various phases of SAP Activate and how agile concepts are used in these phases. We will also cover industry best practices during a discussion of various concepts.

Structuring the explore phase

We have already discussed the phases of SAP Activate in the previous chapters. Let's take a closer look at the explore phase and map it to agile. With the explore phase, SAP Activate facilitates frequent inspection that allows the project team to check customer expectations and build a baseline. It also facilitates the fast demonstration of SAP standards and performs early visualization. The main idea is to create a business value focused backlog. Let's see each sub-component of the explore phase one by one (we will only look at the agile perspective).

One of the key blocks of the explore phase is a solution validation workshop. With a solution validation workshop, it is possible to:

- Perform early adaptation of sprint principles
- Perform a solution demo
- Create a solution documentation produced in Sprints and organized through a business process hierarchy
- Visualization of solution
- Align design approach with business values

- Prioritize product backlogs
- Learn documentation templates:

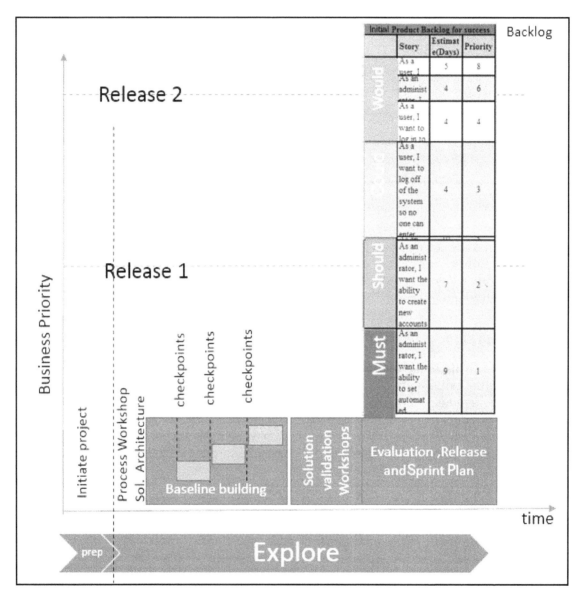

Structuring the explore phase

A baseline build is the starting point and an early opportunity for a business buy-in and feedback. The main objective of a baseline system is to demonstrate the SAP standard (a solution demo approach), verify the SAP standard process, define and agree on a baseline scope, build a baseline system with the company data and structure, identify business requirements, identify initial solution gaps/deltas (initial backlog), and refine the process scope and solution architecture. With an **Iterative baseline build**, we can build a baseline system for solution validation workshops. Just for our understanding and clarity between baseline build and prototype, let's define prototype.

A prototype is a simple experimental model of a proposed solution used to test or validate ideas and design assumptions, and other aspects of its conceptualization quickly and cheaply so that the designer/s involved can make appropriate refinements or possible changes in direction. Prototypes can take many forms, and the only thing the various forms have in common is that they are all tangible forms of your ideas.

To summarize, the main objectives of an Iterative baseline build are as follows:

- Demo SAP standard
- Buy-in for SAP standard/best practices
- Verify processes and scope
- Build a baseline system for solution validation workshop

To check the progress of the baseline build, the explore phase has a **baseline build checkpoint**. It has the following objectives:

- It acts as a mini-review for process owners to show progress
- It is used as an opportunity to explain how SAP standard works
- As a rule of thumb, checkpoints should be planned every two weeks

We have already discussed workshop A and B in detail earlier in `Chapter 3`, *Use Case Scenario for SAP Activate*. Here, we will reiterate the main objective and see how it embraces agile concepts:

- **Workshop A**: With workshop A, the project team identifies delta requirements and gaps. The motto should be to listen, learn, challenge, and complement. Its main objectives are as follows:
    - Identify the gap
    - Challenge to drive improvements/drive SAP standard

- Complement process models delivered through predefined content
- Capture and verify requirements (for example, what do you need to do? How does that work? Why is that important?)
- Determine the process owner
- Associate measures (PPIs)
- Close the loop to the business case

The toolset and methodology used during the workshop A are Solution Manager (for business process hierarchy), modeling toolset, and visualization tools.

Similarly, the main objectives of Workshop B can be jotted down as follows:

- **Workshop B**: It facilitates visualization of solution design for functional gaps and its main objectives are as follows:
    - Visualize solution design for functional gaps
    - Distribute visualization for feedback
    - Refine requirement based on feedback
    - Update requirements documentation in Solution Manager
    - Drive early approval
    - Expect iteration

The toolset and methodology used during the workshop B are irises and visualization techniques of SAP Activate.

The following image summarizes the various components of the explore phase: the input /output, users, and stakeholders involved. As we can clearly see in the image, customer approval happens at the solution validation workshop, and release and Sprint planning thereby help in getting buy-in as early as the explore phase of the project:

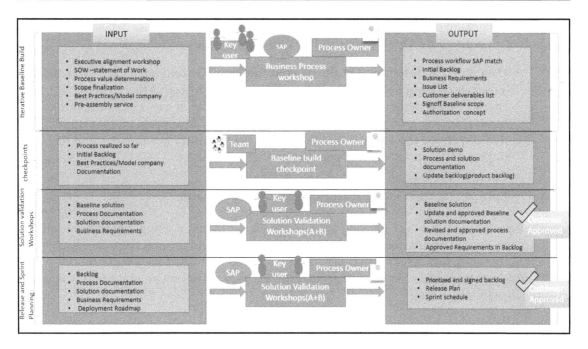

Key components of the explore phase

Creating a product backlog

As discussed in Chapter 4, *Understanding Agile and Scrum*, the product backlog is a list of user stories (requirements) for implementing a product vision. It is a dynamic prioritized requirements list; the details vary by the priority of the requirement (the requirement list gets detailed as the team gets closer to implementing them). The product owner is responsible for it.

Since the product backlog is one of the most important components, it's very important to also know what it is not. The product backlog is not:

- A requirement specification with loads of details
- A list of activities of how to transform requirement into product
- A design documentation

The product backlog provides various levels of detail; the level of details depends on the position of an entry within the scrum product backlog. They are as follows:

- **User story**: A description of the desired functionality told from the perspective of a user or customer. A user story is a very easy yet powerful tool to bring in change that is demanded by the ground-level people. It acts as a multisource input from the ground level team/users. There may be a problem that is not floating on the top and hence, this also gives us an introspection of them to improve the overall service/product in a Sprint fashion.
- **Theme**: A collection of related user stories.
- **Epic**: A large user story, typically a process or scenario.

Once the preliminary product backlog is built, the team can begin using it in their iterative Sprint planning and Sprint execution cycles. As the project evolves and the team discovers more requirements, new user stories will be added and the product backlog will continuously change. This is a normal occurrence and it does not mean that there was any mistake in team's planning.

While the product owner has the final authority and responsibility for managing the product backlog, the whole team provides input to the backlog. Together, the team determines how much work can be done from the backlog for each Sprint iteration. A Sprint planning session is used to determine the number of user stories the team believes they can accomplish in upcoming Sprints, depending on the capabilities of the team and the estimates of user stories in the priority order. The only discipline and control required are picking the right set of user stories and prioritizing them appropriately.

Carefully managed product backlogs are integral to the successful completion of a project and delivery of a product. The backlog requires frequent input from all team members as well as stakeholders/customers. Frequent interaction with the team and stakeholders/customers is one of the tenants of the agile methodology. This ensures that the customer helps the team throughout the planning and execution of the project and receives the product it wants.

The following chart represents how a part of a product backlog may look like--we take an example from an HR system, where new features for payroll need to be implemented.

The product backlog for the new HR system (payroll) is as follows:

Task ID	Story	Estimate	Priority
6	As an employee, I want to enter my work hours so that I can make sure that I get paid on time	6	1
1	As a people manager, I want to approve time sheets so that employees get paid	3	2
3	As an employee, I want to log into the system so that I can perform payroll functions	5	3
2	As an employee, I want to log off the system so that no one can enter erroneous information in my account	6	4
4	As a finance consultant, I want the ability to create new accounts so that we can add employees after they're hired	8	5
7	As a finance consultant, I want to run consolidated payroll reports so that I can provide a weekly status to senior management	9	6
8	As an employee, I want the ability to edit my time sheet so that I can correct any mistakes	6	7
9	As a finance consultant, I want the ability to set automated reminders so that employees will verify and sign their time sheets on time	8	8
5	As a finance manager, I want the ability to archive time sheets so that the organization can file them for audit and tax purposes	15	9

Prioritize the backlog

Agile projects teams rely on prioritized backlog to guide their work. The process owner must prioritize and force the rank list to all requirements in the project backlog. The main reason to have a prioritized backlog is to prevent all items being marked as must have.

The following are the points to note during prioritization of a backlog:

- Rank the backlog continuously
- No two items can end up being equal on the list
- Once you have committed to an iteration plan, you should not change the rank of these committed items
- All other items can be re-ranked whenever you learn new information, usually in the form of feedback or information gathered from the team or stakeholders
- The **must have, should have, could have, and would have** (**MSCW**) priority serves as the starting step; the next step is ranking within the same group priority
- One should keep the impact of prioritizing on other stories
- Time, cost, and risk estimation should be kept in mind during the activity
- Dependencies and integration must be considered

Techniques for prioritization

The product owner must rank the backlog, deciding which story is first, which is second, and so on.

We always start with MSCW and then individually rank each item in the backlog. A story should be broken into multiple child stories if it contains various components. Comparative assessment should be done between selected requirements. Planning poker * can also be used for estimates.

Planning poker is an agile estimating and planning technique that is consensus-based. To start a poker planning session, the product owner or customer reads an agile user story or describes a feature to the estimators. Each member has a deck of planning poker cards with values 0, 1, 2, 3, 5, 8, 13, 20, 40, and 100. The values represent the number of story points, idea days, or other units in which the team estimates. Each feature is discussed and the team members select the card (vote). If the card values of all are the same, then that card value becomes the estimate. Otherwise, it is discussed again. It is repetitive in nature and is continued until a consensus is met.

Using planning poker for SAP projects

If the team members have a similar background and can understand each other, we can use the standard way of planning poker. However, and mostly the common situation, team members are from different backgrounds and cannot judge each other's estimations. In such cases, we need to add additional steps. Once each team member (estimator) has selected a card (score), all cards are turned over at the same time except for the card from the expert (topic/story). His card will be turned over last, and only in the case where the estimates are not the same, the group discusses the estimates focusing only on outlying values and understanding the reasoning behind each other's estimate. The expert then explains his estimates and brings insights. Other steps of planning poker are conducted as is.

The following is a template from SAP that is used across projects by consultants for estimation (for SAP projects):

Man days	➡	Story Points
1. Decide what type of work to include in the estimate		
2.For starter : 1 Person day = 1 Story Point		
3.Select user stories that equal 2 story points		• Short List : Select all stories
4.Select user stories that equal 2 story points		• Long List :Select three stories
5.Select anchor point for 2 and 20 story points by determining which story is most definitely 2,and which is most definitely 20		
6.Depending on the type of project and the number of user stories,decide whether to poker all of them or just the ones you hope to deliver in the next sprint		
7. No previous estimates available : Look at all user stories and determine how they compare to the anchor points		Previous estimates available: Look at all user stories and discuss whether to round up or down to the nearest poker value

Template for estimation

A project needs a common definition of ready and done. The user stories go through stages from new to ready to done. At the minimum, each project has to define what ready and done means. It is a shared definition and compact between terms and stakeholders:

- **Definition of done**: This ideally represents "potentially releasable" or even released state. Done means acceptance criteria are met, cleared by QA, accepted by tactical and strategic PO, integrated, automated testing in place, user documentation created, and Ops documentation created. This definition of done ensures transparency and quality fit for the product and organization. Many teams also make use of a visual task-tracking tool in the form of a wall-sized task board, where tasks (written on post-it notes) migrate during the Sprint across columns labeled: "To Do," "Doing," and "Done."

  In a typical IT project, the team will only deliver products that satisfy; for example, the software has been developed or configured, it works technically and functionally correct, appropriate documentation is done, and quality gates acceptance for operations has been done.

- **Definition of ready**: It means that stories must be immediately actionable. A ready item should be clear, feasible, and testable. The item is moved into Sprints only when it's ready. Typically, stories are ready when they are on the corporate backlog, the project team understands the problem, the team understands why it is important, the story has been estimated and the team can prepare a demo for the product owner, acceptance criteria for the product owner are clear and agreed upon, and acceptance criteria for operations are clear and agreed upon.
- **Definition of shippable**: A potentially shippable product is the sum of the product backlog item delivered each Sprint. The team goes live with the product only when the organization is ready to use the new software, quality assurance has accepted the software, and the acceptance criteria from operations are met:

Ready	Done
- Responsibility of product owner	- Responsibility of Team
- Checked by team	- Checked by product owner
- Indicated that the story is ready for inclusion in a sprint	- Definition of DONE is typically different for story,epic,and release
- Story needs to be	- Definition of DONE spells –out the attributes of the story, epic or release when it is considered complete
- Business priority established	
- Story defined and understandable to the team	
- Small enough to fit into the sprint	
- Contains acceptance criteria	

Comparison between ready and done

To move the product backlog from ready to done status, we run multiple Sprints in iteration until the product increment is potentially shippable:

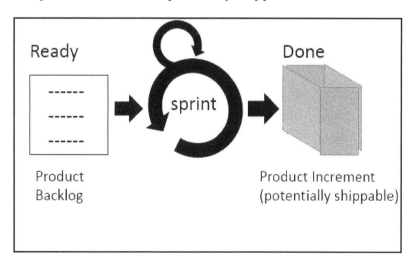

From ready to done

To get the user stories ready, product backlog refinement sessions (also called grooming) and spikes are conducted. Details and estimates are added to the product backlog, and the product backlog for upcoming Sprints are reviewed by the product owner and team. Ready and real user stories are worked in parallel. Tasks are defined to make the user story ready. The team should have sufficient user stories ready for 2-3 Sprints.

The definition for done for Sprint and for release should be clear and the same across the team. Done for Sprint refers to activity in the development environment (in perspective of IT), for example, a solution built and configured in the development system, the solution is tested by process owner and tester, bugs fixed, and functionality transported to a quality system for acceptance test. While the definition of done for release implies functionalities ready for release to business, for example, user acceptance tested, integration tested, training material completed, and so on.

Story mapping for SAP projects

Story mapping is a top-down approach to requirement gathering. It arranges user stories into a useful model that is easy to understand and allows you tell your user story in a simpler way. It helps you identify missing details (if any) in your backlog and effectively plan the release.

In general, the story map structure looks as follows:

In a SAP Project perspective, we can redraw it as follows:

Now, let's see how the structure of a story flows. As depicted in the following image, we start with Epic Business Context (scenario) and break it down further into processes and process steps:

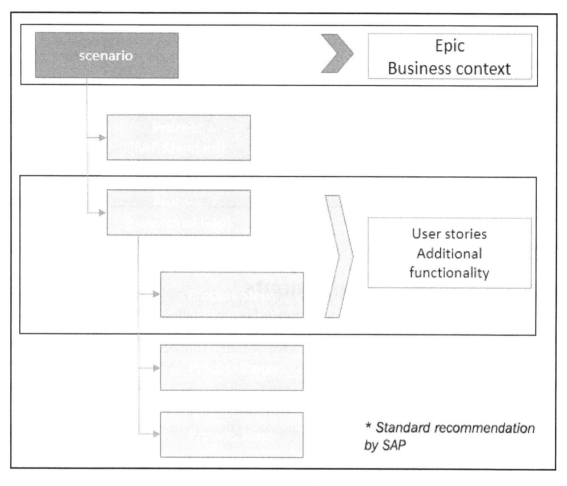

Story map structure flow in a SAP context

For example, plan to produce -> demand management -> forecast product demand.

Let's see what a user story looks like in a scrum model and in a SAP Project:

Scrum	SAP Project(using SAP Activate)
- User oriented format - As a <ROLE > i want <ACTION> so that I can <GOAL>	- Captures headline and short description of the requirement in the product backlog - Streamlined Templates - Easy to capture the requirements for teams familiar with SAP Activate Templates - SAP requirement document

User story format

Non-functional requirements

A common challenge while writing a user story is how to handle a product's non-functional requirements. These are requirements that are not about a specific functionality but rather about operational qualities, such as performance, security, and technical requirements. These are normally captured as performance constraints. Scrum teams have been putting NFR as stories in the backlog and it has worked for them.

A product owner can define the overall story/epic that may be large and would require decomposing into Sprintable stories. These are stories that can be understood, estimated, and are small enough to fit into the Sprint. It's done over the project progressively.

While working with backlog, we should keep the following points in mind:

- Flat backlog is hard to work with
- SAP historically relies on business process maps
- User story mapping is a very common concept—solution maps or business process maps provide input to story mapping
- A user story map drives prioritization and release and Sprint planning

Defining project scope

Any project ideally starts with questions about the problem that we want to solve with the project. A proper definition of a project scope at the start of a project makes life much easier for the project team. Defining project scope is driven by three questions:

- What do you want to achieve and why? (This is basically the vision of the project.)
- What are the processes in scope?
- Who needs it? (This helps to create the user story.)

For example, one of the recent projects done by us was data-driven sales. The vision for this project was "Support sales force and customer services in interactive selling." The solution will prevent business blindness of responsible sales representatives, strengthen existing customer relationship during reviews, and give them means to quickly respond to competitor's activities. The processes in scope were sales planning and forecasting, customer contact management, opportunity management, and contract management. We were targeting it for sales managers, contract managers, account managers, and customers:

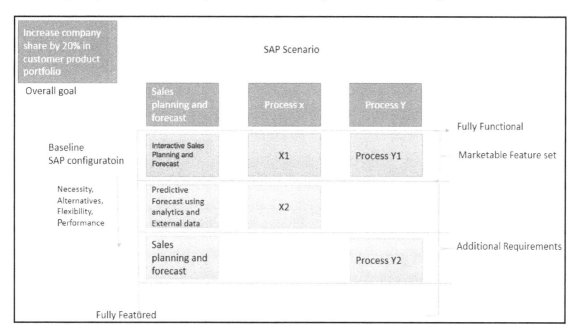

Story mapping (SAP's way)

Understanding estimation and planning of your projects

Estimating and planning are critical to the success of software development irrespective of the projects size. The agile teams usually use the planning onion concept. They plan at least at the release, iteration, and day level. Release planning considers the user stories that will be developed for a new release of a product or system. It determines an appropriate answer to the questions of scope, schedule, and resources for a projects. Release planning occurs at the start of a projects.

During iteration planning, we talk about the tasks that will be needed to transform a feature request into a working and tested software.

Most agile teams use the daily stand-up meeting to coordinate work and synchronize daily efforts. It might seem excessive to consider this planning in a formal sense; teams make, assess, and revise their plans during these meetings:

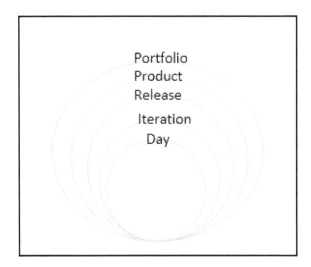

Planning onion

Planning is preceded by estimating (estimating the resources, time, and size) required to develop a user story, features, or requirement. For example, to estimate the size we should consider:

- **Story point**: Unit of measurement for expressing the overall size of a user story, features, or other pieces of work. What matters are the relative values related to how hard it is and how much of there is, not related to the amount of time or number of people. Choose a medium size story and assign it a value 8. Use this as a reference and estimate other stories as—twice big or half, as shown in the following example:

```
0 , 1 , 2 , 3 , 5 , 8 , 13 , 20 , 40 , 100
```
Near term iteration "stories"   A few iteration away Epic

- **Idea time**: The amount of time something takes when stripped of all peripheral activities. When estimating idea day, it is assumed that the story being estimated is the only thing you will work on; there will be no interruption.
- **Elapsed time**: The amount of time that passes while doing something.
- **Velocity**: Measure of a team's rate of progress. It is calculated by summing the number of story points assigned to each user story that the team completed during the operation. Since all user stories are estimated relative to each other, its velocity should change and not each story point estimate, for future releases.

The following is an overview of a high-level release planning. We have already discussed the projects backlog definition and projects backlog prioritization--the responsibility for which lies with the product owner. The **Implementation Team** checks for cross-functional requirements and analyzes the technical dependencies. So, once a product owner states that a requirement is of high priority to him, the **Implementation Team** analyzes the business requirement and related technical prerequisites into the backlog. All the technical prerequisites for the process must automatically have priority and should be taken into consideration for release and Sprint planning.

Estimating projects backlog is the responsibility of the **Implementation Team**; they use two units of estimation—idea person days and story points/relative size. Teams also use planning poker to estimate an story. This estimate covers all activities to a point of completion of Sprint and release:

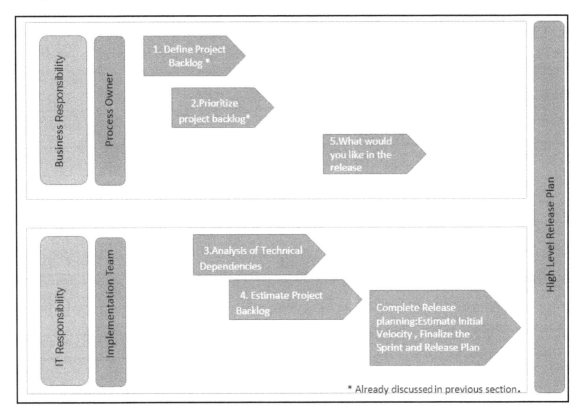

High-level overview of release planning

The process owner is responsible for deciding what will be shipped in the release. Typically, it is scope driven (functionality) and budget driven (timeline). The process owner must decide which requirement from the projects backlog needs to be realized so that the business can gain benefit, keeping in mind when the business expects the first release. He also takes into consideration the budget constraints. In agile projects, the release planning is value driven.

The scrum master and the team are responsible for velocity definition. *Average velocity = Sum of N previous Sprint velocities/N*. Initial velocity is always an estimate and it is fine tuned over the next few Sprints. This should always be taken into consideration while planning. The release plan is completed with estimate initial velocity, finalizing the Sprint and release plan:

Release 1	start	Sprint 1	Sprint 2	Sprint 3	Sprint 4	Sprint 5	Sprint 6
Forecast : Work remaining at start of sprint		180	170	147	116	90	76
Actual: Work remaining at start of sprint		180	168	145	110	76	0
Forecast :Velocity		30	35	40	42	42	42
Actual : Velocity		35	35	36			
Forecast:changed Estimates		10	5	3	3		
Actual changed Estimates		10	4	2	4		
Forecast : Points from new requirements		8	6	6	6		
Actual Points from new requirements		18	8	6	4		
Forecast : Work remaining at the end of sprint	180	170	147	116	90		0
Actual Work remaining at the end of sprint	180	168	145	110	76		

Release planning

Sprint cycles and their importance

Sprint is a 2-4 week of timebox of work during which—analysis, design, code, and the test is performed. Each Sprint has a little bit of all. A typical Sprint cycle looks as follows:

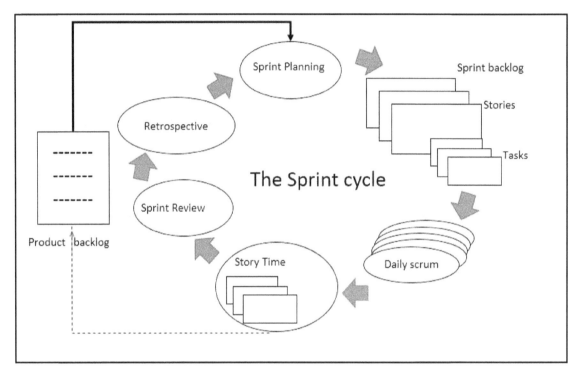

Sprint cycle

The Sprint execution inside the Sprint cycle will have a structure as shown in the following image, that is, it will have a design, build test, and document steps for all the delta requirements. So, at a given moment, for a user story X, Y, Z, and R, we will see this:

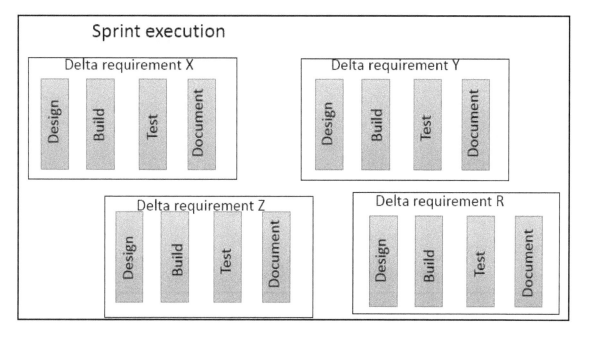

The following is the overview of the iterative realize phase of SAP Activate. SAP Activate (realize) uses the agile philosophy of Sprints and iterative build:

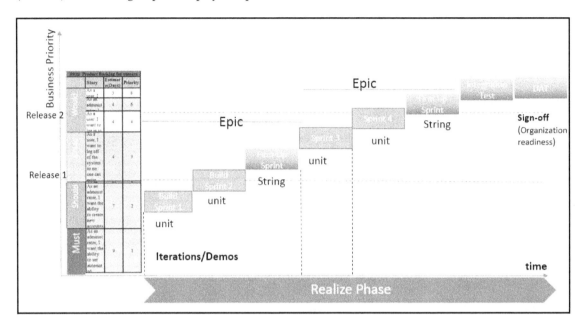

Iterative realize phase of SAP Activate

Deploy your solution

Before we think of deploying the solution, it is very important to ensure that the solution is consumable. We need to make sure that the solution is technically ready to be deployed and stakeholders are ready to accept the solution. Once assured of this, we can prepare for deployment. The cut-over team decides and finalizes what activities are needed to deploy the solution and how to define the criteria for a successful deployment:

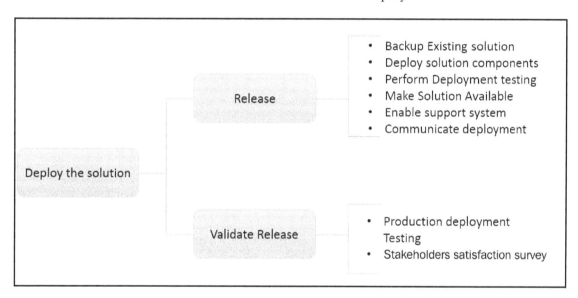

Solution deployment

Let's quickly revisit the overview of steps about deployment and support in SAP Activate (already discussed in Chapter 4, *Understanding Agile and Scrum*):

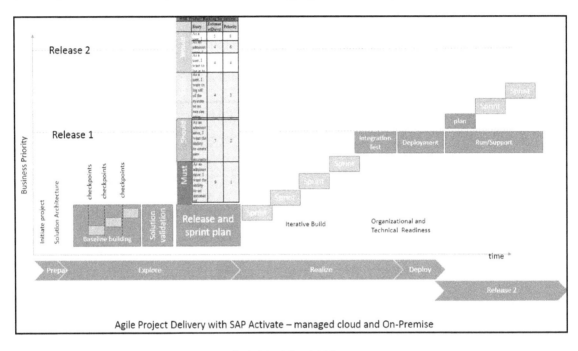

Sap Activate - Agile project delivery

Deployment of the solution is preceded by testing. The test strategy is delivered in the explore phase (SAP Activate) and reviewed by technical and functional teams. An overview of solution testing activities throughout the projects can be summarized as follows:

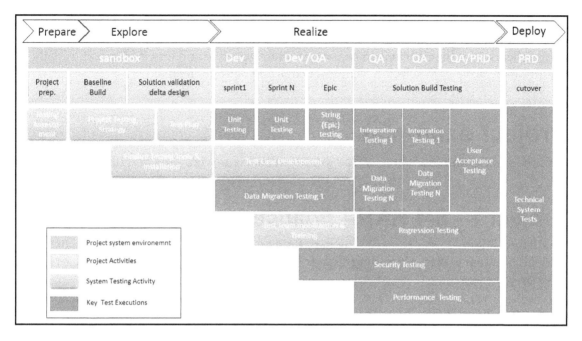

Solution testing across different phases of SAP Activate

In the realization phase, unit testing is done for each build Sprint in the development environment. Once the epic is complete, string testing is also done. In the same phase (realization), integration testing is done before user acceptance testing as solution build testing. Sap Activate provides a number of templates and accelerators for each test scenarios and various business processes.

Once the testing is complete and the solution is approved in the quality system, SAP Activate supports and facilitates templates to perform cutover and transition. These templates are readily available in the SAP JAM portal.

The deploy phase can also be performed in Sprints. The cutover planning meeting can be organized like a scrum meeting, assigning cut-over activities to the cut-over user stories. A dress rehearsal for the cutover can be used as a retrospective and lessons learned. A daily scrum can be done with selected technical teams and cut-over teams.

Project examples

Let's see some examples, where earlier discussed concepts were used and implemented.

Project 1 - S/4 HANA finance implementation

Challenge: The customer was running very tight on timelines. This means that it would be difficult for them to start everything from scratch and also had no time and resources to develop test plans.

Realized benefit

- Used model company
- Proof of concept project proved the feasibility and benefit of method used, refined the business needs and technological limitation, and paved a way for an IT project

Project scope

- Implement data lake for the data science team using SAP HANA, SAP Vora, Hadoop, Spark, and other tools
- One of the sources for the data lake was SAP S/4 HANA system

Implementation approach

- Used the SAP Activate methodology with agile accelerators
- Used scrum-based approach to implement the solution

Project 2 - Moving from legacy system to SAP SuccessFactors

The company was using a legacy system and wanted to move to SAP SuccessFactors.

Realized benefit

- Customer satisfaction in business was involved right from day one.
- The transition from the legacy system to a new environment was smooth as it was incremental. Business disruption was minimized.

Project scope

- HR system, manager self-service, and employee self-service
- Region-wise rollout of the solution

Iterative build and incremental approach

- The core team was based out of one central work location
- Used scrum-based approach to implement the solution
- Concepts such as planning poker were used for story score
- Workshop A and Workshop B were performed for solution validation and gap analysis

- Templates and accelerators were used to jump-start the projects:

High-level plan with timelines for the project

Project 3 - Proof of concept for data lake

Challenge: As the requirement was not clear when the project team started, it was very much important for the team to use a methodology that was flexible enough to allow a change in requirement over time and encourage constant feedback from end users.

Realized benefit

- Built prototype using iterative approach to clarify requirements as the technology and business need was not clarified at the start of the project
- Proof of concept project proved feasibility and benefit of method used, refined the business needs and technological limitations, and paved a way for an IT project

Project scope

- Implemented data lake for the data science team using SAP HANA, SAP Vora, Hadoop, Spark, and other tools
- One of the sources for the data lake was the SAP S/4 HANA system

Implementation approach

- Used the SAP Activate methodology with agile accelerators
- Used scrum-based approach to implement the solution

Summary

In this chapter, we discussed examples from different projects and industry best practices that might help you in your projects. You learned how phases of SAP Activate embraces agile concepts and makes SAP projects more agile than traditional methodologies. Concepts such as the planning poker and onion model were introduced to make planning and estimation simpler. We extended our discussion from structuring the prepare phase to deploying the solution, discussing and understanding various components and building blocks involved in the process.

This brings us to the end of the book; by now, you should be comfortable with the methodology and framework related to SAP Activate and how to use SAP Activate as the next generation scrum tool for project management.

Test yourself

(More than one answer may be correct)

1. Scrum allows for re-estimating tasks based on growing insights. Which scrum team member is responsible for updating the estimates of the work during the Sprint?
    - Development team
    - Scrum master
    - Product owner
    - None of this

2. Who are involved in the scrum?
    - Development team
    - Scrum master
    - Product owner
    - None of this

3. What are the artifacts of the scrum?
    - Sprint backlog
    - Product backlog
    - Velocity chart
    - All of this

4. What kind of software development projects can be executed by a scrum framework?
    - Customer projects
    - Complete software packages
    - All kinds of software development
    - None of this

5. Where are the customer requirements stored?
    - Product backlog
    - Sprint backlog
    - Database
    - With scrum product owner

6. What is important for all scrum projects?
    - Self-organization
    - Clear hierarchy in the company
    - Communication
    - Continuous improvement

Index